THE **BIG IDEA** BOOK

THE BIG IDEA BOOK

**Five hundred new ideas
to change the world
in ways big and small**

www.idea-a-day.com

info@idea-a-day.com

CAPSTONE

658
1467258

Idea A Day Ltd. 2004

The right of Dave Owen to be identified as the author of this work has been asserted in accordance with the Copyright, Designs and Patents Act 1988

First published 2004 by
Capstone Publishing Limited (A Wiley Company)
The Atrium, Southern Gate, Chichester,
West Sussex PO19 8SQ, United Kingdom
www.wileyeurope.com

CIP catalogue records for this book are available from the British Library and the US Library of Congress

ISBN 1-84112-565-2

Designed and typeset by Baseline, Oxford, UK
Printed and bound by T.J. International Ltd, Padstow, Cornwall
This book is printed on acid-free paper

Substantial discounts on bulk quantities of Capstone books are available to corporations, professional associations and other organizations. For details telephone Jphn Wiley & Sons on (+44 1243 770441) or fax (+44 1243 770571) or e-mail CorporateDevelopment@wiley.co.uk

10 9 8 7 6 5 4 3 2 1

CONTENTS

FOREWORD

I love this book. (No surprise, since they decided to print my foreword.)

You might be surprised, though, to know *why* I love this book. I don't love it because of all the juicy ideas herein. Some of the ideas are great, naturally, while others are pretty dodgy.

What I love is how many ideas there are. What I love is the fact that every single day for more than 1,000 days, a new idea has shown up in my email inbox. This is proof positive that we've got more ideas than we know what to do with. Proof that your idea, no matter how great it is, can't possibly be much better than all of the ideas in this book. And these ideas are free, for God's sake!

The lessons are simple. First, stop keeping your idea a secret. Ideas in secret die. They need light and air or they starve to death. The more people you share your idea with, the more likely it is to become real.

The second lesson is even more important – it's not the idea that matters, it's what you do with it. The real challenge (and the real skill) comes from championing your idea, shepherding it through the system and turning it into a reality.

So, here's my challenge: pick an idea, any idea. From this book or the one you've been carrying around like a fragile egg. Now go do something with it. Tell people about it. Share it. Build a prototype. Launch it cheap.

Make something happen. You can do it.

Seth Godin
Author of *Purple Cow*

THE REVIEW PANEL

In preparing the five hundred ideas published in this book, the Idea A Day team assembled a review committee of respected individuals. The committee members were invited to comment freely on the ideas. Their feedback helped shape the final selection.

The authors would like to thank:

Richard Bacon, television presenter

David Brook, founder of Optimistic Media

James Brown, founder and publisher of *Loaded* and *Jack*

Charles Cohen, entrepreneur

Tim Coulson, Marketing Director of Ministry of Sound

William Egleton, writer and artist

Pete Fowler, graphic artist

Toby Gunton, Director of Dowcarter, Digital Marketing Communications Agency

Wayne Hemingway, father of four and designer

Annabel Hills, CEO Lucky Pants

Ken Langdon, author of *The 100 Greatest Business Ideas of All Time*

Liam Lynch, musician and film director

Tim Maguire, creative and commercials director

Jay Pond-Jones, Head of Content, Flipside Television

Christopher Satterthwaite, Chief Executive of Chime Communications

Alex Smith, video director

INTRODUCTION

By David Owen

I have always had a lot of ideas. Too many ideas perhaps. Sometimes these ideas seemed so promising and compelling that plans were drawn up to make them a reality. For the most part, however, the ideas disappeared as quickly as they had materialised, providing nothing more than a brief mental diversion – they were either too crazy to take seriously or too big to consider tackling. In truth, even those concepts that were both exciting and achievable eventually fizzled out or got sidelined when another five new ideas came along. Between the ages of 18 and 28, I must have started a hundred projects. I have business plans, letters to company directors and half-finished novels littering the hard drives of now defunct Amstrad PCWs and Mac Classics. I spent ten years scribbling notes, talking non-stop, expanding on ideas and putting teams of people together. And I had nothing to show for it. I didn't actually achieve anything.

When I had the idea for the Idea A Day website in January 2000, I was as relieved as I was excited. Finally, I had an idea that went some way to solving my problem rather than adding to it. Too many ideas? Well, now I would publish an original idea every day on the Internet. We will see how far too many can really go! Thank God for that. And thank God for the Internet.

First steps
The Idea A Day concept had surfaced before 2000. I remember meeting up with a friend called Justin Cooke in 1997. We had been at college in

Manchester together where we had launched a magazine (one issue and no more); he had staged a film festival (that is still an annual event, I believe). Justin proved to be more a doer of things than I ever was (in '97 he was just about to found Fortune Cookie, the web agency that would later build the Idea A Day website) but he wasn't short of ideas either. We were meeting because he wanted to discuss a concept he had for Pop Paints – paint colours mixed by pop stars and targeted at kids. In response, I had come up with a range of paints and soft furnishings inspired by impressionist paintings. We were supposed to be planning an approach to the paint companies or DIY chains to progress these concepts. What we actually did was think of another idea completely – an exhibition of disposable cameras with which artists and celebrities would have taken pictures but not had them exposed. We liked this idea so much that we had some great business cards designed. I still have five hundred of them, boxed and unopened.

I also remember discussing the problem of having too many ideas and not being able to do any of them. For a while we planned to compose a page of our ideas and fax them for free to companies we wanted to work with. We half thought and half hoped that if we sent a fax every month, the recipient companies would eventually come back to us – either to develop the ideas we gave them or to ask us to generate more, on an exclusive basis. We never sent any faxes. I don't think we were as confident about the free delivery concept as we were about some of the ideas themselves. I also think that we both knew that the facsimile was the wrong medium for the message. But that was, at least, the precursor to the 'big idea'.

When I finally came up with the Internet version of Idea A Day, I was working quite happily for EMI Music Publishing. It was my job to promote the use of EMI's one and a half million songs in commercials, television and films. I had found my way into this career after leaving Manchester with a drama degree, opening a shop in my home town of Portsmouth, working as a media journalist, and finally editing a magazine about advertising. EMI wanted me because I knew a lot of ad people and, to some degree, knew what they were about. If anyone was going to twist an art director or copywriter's arm to use a song by the Velvet Underground, or The Fall, or even Leo Sayer, it was me. It was a great job, but it was also a limiting one. EMI is a big company with a number of interests but they weren't in a hurry to start manufacturing Sweet Teeth, the kid's mint confectionery in the shape of molars and incisors, or any of the other concepts that continually distracted me from the job in hand. The real fun that I had, and perhaps the real work that I did, was hanging out with advertising creatives and commercials' directors, and talking about ideas.

The eventual website concept – to publish an original idea every day on the Internet for free – was, in all honesty, as much born of vanity as anything else. At 28, I was really beginning to feel under-appreciated and was craving respect for what I saw as my fairly unusual talent for constantly thinking of new ideas. The business world is not set up to greatly value individuals with too many ideas. Having one good idea and pursuing it through hard work and some talent is the favoured model for success amongst entrepreneurs and venture capitalists. And if there were jobs that required nothing more than the candidate to think of new concepts all the time, I was not aware of them. In response to what I then considered to be a gaping hole in the fabric of society, I set out to think of a great idea every day. I was challenging myself. If I could pull it off, I thought, surely someone will be sufficiently impressed to offer me a job or sink some money into at least one of the ideas.

The team

The first 50 ideas I scribbled down were largely drawn from the ten years I had spent trying to do something with them all. I remember walking around Soho on lunch breaks and calling my voicemail with every idea I could remember. When I got back to my desk, there would be four or five ideas to type up. After a few weeks of this activity, I was getting very eager to publish them. Justin Cooke had agreed to have Fortune Cookie build the site in return for a stake in the venture, but it would still take months to design and get online. Unable to wait for the positive feedback I craved, I began emailing ideas to people I respected in the hope that they would be suffieciently impressed to offer me immediate and lavish praise. I remember emailing pages of ideas to Wayne Hemingway, whom I had met when selling design reference materials to him at Red or Dead (how else?) and to Chas Bayfield, an advertising creative who had written some of the best commercials for Tango. Wayne sent the pages back with notes on how to progress the ideas, who I should talk to, and who might be interested. Like Justin Cooke, Wayne is a doer of things, and very impressive with it. Chas, though, took a different tack. For every idea I sent him, he sent others back — 50 of them. I had found a partner, and just as importantly, I was on the cusp of sharing my biggest idea (now www.idea-a-day.com) with another two people... and, ultimately, with the entire global online community (in principle at least!).

It was Chas who introduced me to the other two partners in Idea A Day. Becky Clarke was another ad creative — or rather, she wasn't just another ad creative, she was one of the least pretentious and most pragmatic I had ever met. Becky had met Chas when working as a receptionist at HHCL and Partners (the advertising agency of the '90s, as determined by *Campaign* magazine). Becky and Chas struck up a rapport and collaborated on many projects, including a T-shirt made out of tea towels that Chas wore to work on a regular basis. Becky was clearly crazy enough to design the shirt but not daft enough to wear it. Now a creative director at the agency Quiet Storm, Becky's ideas have always been more purposeful than fanciful and all the more welcome for it.

Quite refreshingly, Rupert Kaye had never worked in advertising. When we started Idea A Day, he was the deputy head of a primary school in Richmond and had previously been the manager of a Drive Thru McDonald's. Chas and Rupert had operated as a two-man think-tank for many years. They met at university in Birmingham and shared a bedsit in London in the years following. The way they tell it, the pair of them thought of ambient advertising, virtual reality and Internet shopping years before anyone knew what they were talking about. That neither of them has come up with anything quite so impressive in the three years that Idea A Day has been running should not, of course, prompt anyone to doubt their story. Rupert, who has since been appointed Chief Executive of the Association of Christian Teachers, has consistently proved to be the most idealistic of us all. His ideas, whether for restoring the ancient wonders of the world or building a replica of Noah's Ark, are often grand gestures designed to make the world a better place. That he also thought of an amusingly flawed idea for an A to Z supermarket, in which all the goods would be arranged in alphabetical order (this idea was never published), was probably just as crucial a factor in his joining the team.

Ideas as entertainment

Through numerous idea sessions and planning meetings, we came to realise that the ideas − in the way they were written or told, or in their consideration and discussion − were entertaining. While it would have been great if all the ideas could have been realised (the products designed and released, the marketing plans actioned, or the policies implemented), we also recognised that the concepts themselves had a certain currency. Some were funny, some were thought-provoking and many were both. We liked ideas in the same way that we liked songs, or paintings, or films. We were dangerously close to becoming an ideas club rather than a company! But that was how the website was launched.

Idea A Day got off to a flying start. Within a couple of weeks of the first idea being published in August 2000, we had reviews and articles printed in various newspapers and magazines, including *The Independent*, *The Express* and *The Daily Telegraph*. The number of subscribers to the daily email leapt to one thousand (and has steadily risen ever since). The interest, particularly that of the press, was focused specifically on the *idea* of ideas being given away. I used the phrase 'wilfully stupid' in a press release to explain our copyright-free stance, although I am sure many other commentators and entrepreneurs would have been happy with just the latter word of that phrase. It was the time of the dotcom boom, of plentiful venture capital and fortunes being made overnight. Each and every new idea (however ill-formed) for the Internet or technology in general, was highly prized and guarded. Everything anyone could think of was worth a million pounds or even a hundred million pounds. Idea A Day's profligacy with ideas, and good ideas for the most part, seemed to be nonsensical. But the anti-commercial stance was also our unique selling point; it made for good copy and caught the public imagination. We played up to it, of course. We declared on the homepage that the ideas were copyright free, when in fact they could be nothing else. There is no copyright over an idea or concept — at least not until specific devices, mechanisms or elements are patented or copyrighted in their own right. (In fact we did assign and protect the wording and phrasing of the ideas themselves — lest we should want to syndicate them to other sites, or print them on tea towels and mugs, or publish a book, even.) But, really, we gave the ideas away because we didn't know anyone who would pay for them and didn't have the time or skills to do many of them ourselves. We were also very curious to see what would happen. Our thinking was along the lines of: 'We all have good jobs and are confident of thinking of more ideas the next day, so why the hell not? 'Let's show off a bit!' was probably the final and most motivating thought.

Global assistance

I, of course, was never going to have a good and original idea every day. The four of us together could not have come up with enough ideas to run the site for the rest of our lives. Fortunately, we had added a 'submit an idea' function to the site early on in its design. Idea submissions come in from all over the world on a daily basis and those that we like we publish. This book has many authors and all are credited with the ideas they contributed. There is nothing better when editing Idea A Day than checking the submissions and finding an idea so good that it just walks onto the site. I recall one day when seven great ideas arrived more or less at once. At the time, it felt to me as though the people who sent them in had just handed me a week's holiday.

Naturally, there have been a great many ideas over the years that we have not published. In the early days, most submissions were rejected because we didn't think the ideas were good enough. Some were ludicrously bad and I have always been confident that a book compiling the worst ideas we received would sell far better than this book — not that we have any plans to publish and embarrass anyone. More recently, and certainly after we passed the 1,000-idea mark, most idea submissions have gone unpublished because we had featured them before in one form or another. Having said that, some ideas are rejected now because they aren't good enough and because we had published them before!

Quality control

There have been many days when we have published ideas in the full knowledge that they weren't up to standard. It can get pretty desperate. It's a terrible feeling because we knew that they would get read (the ideas are emailed to thousands of subscribers every day) and that they would disappoint. However, we were also aware that many people would notice the absence of an email on the day if we failed to deliver. I quickly realised the limits of my profligacy after attempting to upload 30 new ideas to cover the site's first Christmas period when I was planning to go away. I just about made it, but the first week of January saw a lot of pacing around and searching phonecalls to friends. In retrospect, it was stupid to commit to publishing on the weekends and idiotic to publish on Christmas Day and Easter Sunday – no one even wants to get an email then anyway. Fortunately, the 500-idea format of this book has given us an opportunity to focus on the ideas – whether written by ourselves or submitted by the public – of which we are most proud.

A source of inspiration

Idea A Day has been received in many different ways. The email subscribers include entrepreneurs, journalists, designers, academics and a great many people who work in advertising. It would be our guess from the responses we have had, that a small number of subscribers are looking for ideas to implement, while the majority are just keen to stay in touch with the modern world – with technology and innovation. People who stay subscribed for more than a month or so, do so because they find the emails entertaining or thought provoking (which for many creatively minded people is much the same thing). That the publication of the ideas seems to act as a spark for readers to come up with more ideas is one of the real joys of Idea A Day. Whether the ideas are near perfect, or flawed, or just plain stupid, they do provide inspiration for further thought. I remember hearing from an acquaintance at the new media venture arm of KPMG, that a 15-minute break would be unofficially taken when each day's idea arrived. The young venture capitalists would discuss the merits of each idea and assess their viability. The ideas used to go out at 10am and within the hour we would often receive an idea or two from staffers at KPMG.

Hotwiring the brain
There are a great many books on the business shelves of bookshops that concern themselves with the creative process. This book is not going to add much to any attempts made thus far to either understand the business of creativity or to teach it to people. That said, this book will inspire a lot of people to have a lot of ideas and it will do so for two reasons.

The first is that the ideas on these pages cover a lot of ground and focus on a very wide variety of subjects, topics or technologies in very few words. The ideas are expressed for the most part in just a few sentences. They are therefore really only summaries of more detailed plans that may or may not exist in the writer's head. They quite often gloss over, or neatly disguise with a joke or turn of phrase, a lot more problems that might arise from their implementation than they might actually solve. But by being incomplete, they are suggestive. They leave gaps that the reader is naturally inclined to fill in. If they are flawed, they invite the reader to correct them. If they work better on the page than they might do in actuality, or are compelling but crazy, the reader can reapply their mechanisms or devices to other problems.

The second reason that this book will be an enabler to creativity is that we have, with these 500 ideas, given 'ideas' a recognisable form and a value distinct from their actual execution. The house style for writing up ideas was determined before the site went live. We felt we needed a consistency of approach so that subscribers would be able to take in each day's idea quickly, without being tripped up or distracted by variations in their delivery. We have, for example, always opened with a verb and always written in the conditional tense. After a few months, submissions began to arrive in this style – which was certainly welcome from an editing point of view. But we did more than suggest a neat way to express tricky concepts: we offered ideas a home.

The value of ideas

It would not be unreasonable to assume that, before Idea A Day (and other idea sites that came before and after us), many of the ideas we published would otherwise have been known only to one or a few people or simply forgotten. Quite a number of submissions to Idea A Day arrive prefaced with a comment to the effect of 'such and such a person suggested I send this to you'. I have personally retrieved some brilliant ideas from other people's quite unassuming conversations. The fact is that people have ideas of value on a regular basis, they just don't recognise them as such. Just like me, people say, 'Wouldn't it be great if...' all the time, and what follows could well be something that the world would benefit from.

The business of ideas was traditionally a very simple matter. People had ideas and people implemented ideas. If an idea wasn't put into practice, it didn't really exist – it held only a potential value. Generally speaking, the ideas, and particularly the good ideas, that went unrealised did so because whoever thought of them didn't have the necessary knowledge, contacts or will to make them happen – and why should they? Even though the counter argument would cite 14 year olds who built huge companies from their bedrooms to suggest that anyone can make something happen if the idea is good and they try hard enough, the fact is that there is no actual reason or law that compels someone with an idea to pursue it for financial gain or a Nobel prize. Idea A Day has gone some way to taking the pressure off creatively minded people. Ideas can have a value in their own right – whether it is to challenge, inspire or entertain those that read or hear them. There is a talent to thinking of ideas that is quite separate from doing anything with them.

Born free

The strapline to Idea A Day was always 'Where ideas are free'. As well as being copyright or royalty free, we always liked the suggestion that the ideas were roaming free – free of the shackles of implementation. This world in which the ideas exist is an odd one. There has always been an element of science fiction at work in Idea A Day, even if the imagined future is more that of tomorrow than the year 3000. Idea A Day offered an alternative reality, with a kind of 'what if?' take on things as they are. In doing so, it provided some form of commentary on its times. Collectively, the 500 ideas published in this book are representative of the way people have been thinking in recent years. The references to specific technologies will tie the book to the years 2000–2004, but one imagines future historians will be just as fascinated by what the writers of this book thought the world lacked at the time. The Big Idea Book could be a history of things that don't exist, if that is not too postmodern a concept to bother pursuing!

Ideas become reality

The question most frequently asked with regard to Idea A Day (other than to ask why we give them away) is whether any of the ideas get taken up and developed. The answer is yes – some of them have found their way into the real world. We can't make a claim to having published the blueprint for an innovation that has been incredibly successful or revolutionalised the modern world. In fact, we wouldn't want to go as far as to suggest that the site has directly inspired anything in particular. There is always the strong possibility that ideas submitted to Idea A Day were either conceived prior to our publication, or would have occurred to someone else completely independently of the site in any case. It may simply have been down to the great pressure of uploading a new idea every day, but we have never allocated any time to tracking or researching the possible development of the ideas. We also designed the site in such a way that the author of each idea could be contacted directly by email, independently of Idea A Day. If anyone other than the site's partners is approached to develop an idea (and such approaches are probably quite common), we wouldn't know about it.

I certainly recall Chas Bayfield campaigning from the outset to publish an idea he had for lemon flavoured cola. Unfortunately, I had misunderstood the concept and was under the illusion that he was proposing an actual slice of lemon to be placed inside each can – which I thought was commercial suicide. When I finally realised that he meant a dash of lemon, I attempted to make up for my mistake, and my rudeness, by allocating the idea one of the Christmas Day slots. About six months later, Coke launched their lemon variety with considerable success. If we had only published a year earlier, Chas might have had more to back up his claim that he inspired the product launch – which, of course, he hadn't at all.

In another example, we published a terrific idea for an alternative emergency number – 888 – which could be used by anyone unsure as to whether their personal dilemma warranted the attentions of the real emergency services. Again, about a year later, we read in *The Mirror* that a local constabulary (in East Anglia, as I remember it) was to trial such an 888 service to relieve pressure on the 999 number. Whether or not the trial was successful, we have no idea. Probably not, or we would have heard more about it.

I also remember publishing an SMS text-based mobile game which combined 'Spin the Bottle' and 'Truth or Dare' – a mobile phone would be spun between a group of friends and whoever it pointed to would text a number for a truth or a dare, which would be returned immediately from a prepared archive. It was a great idea (one of George Cockerill's, the Fortune Cookie information architect who built the site). I knew a few people in the then-emerging ringtones and mobile entertainment business and rang one of them the next day to pitch it to him. He told me that he had not only seen the idea but had in turn called one of the major UK phone operators to pitch it to them. Furthermore, his contact at the operator had quickly informed him that they too had seen the idea on 'a website' and were getting on with it!

The very first idea that we ran – Becky Clarke's 'Keyholders' company, which is also the first idea in this book – became a reality within about four months of our publication. A company sprang up with a similar name and offering a similar service – a house-key depository, which, in their version, could be used to grant access for workmen to a customer's home, as well as being on hand if a customer inadvertently locked themselves out of their own home. The company had a website and a number of their vans were spotted driving around London. That company couldn't have been very successful – the vans quickly disappeared. Personally, I'd like to think that was more a result of a flawed execution than any fault in the original idea, which is still, in my opinion at least, one of the best we have published.

Most of the ideas we have run on the site that have either directly or indirectly materialised following publication have been left out of this book. There were ideas for television formats that may or may not have inspired, or been inspired by, various new programmes – mostly in the reality or quiz genres that exploded after 'Big Brother' and 'Who Wants To Be A Millionaire?'. There were also countless variations on what would become anonymous text chat or text flirting, the advertisements for which suddenly started to fill pages of small ads in 2001.

Thank you

As a final word, we really would like to thank everyone who has submitted ideas to the site. These people are the authors of this book and will hopefully take as much pride in its publication as we do. Of course, our new readers are invited to submit their own ideas to Idea A Day. We all have our sights set on a sequel.

David Owen
Founder of Idea A Day
on behalf of Chas Bayfield, Rupert Kaye and Becky Clarke
www.idea-a-day.com

Open 24-hour key bureaux in major towns and cities at which the public could deposit a spare set of keys for their homes, offices or cars. Customers would pay an annual insurance premium, ensuring the spare keys would be immediately dispatched to them if they found themselves locked out.

Becky Clarke
18 August 2000

Design a baby's plastic bathtub that changes colour according to the temperature of the water (red — too hot; pale green — just right; blue — too cold).

Rupert Kaye
19 August 2000

Open a restaurant called The Ten Floors. The building would be a pyramid – with each floor being smaller than the one below it. The menu and price of meals would become increasingly exotic and expensive on each floor. The highest and most exclusive floor would be popular with ambassadors and kings, while everything on the ground floor would be priced at cost, and designed to appeal to students. A soup kitchen could operate in a bargain basement.

Chas Bayfield
20 August 2000

Curate an art exhibition of disposable cameras with which artists, photographers and other notable individuals have taken pictures but never developed the films. The exhibition would be minimalist in presentation, consisting solely of identical cameras with the artists' names displayed.

David Owen
21 August 2000

Editor's note:
We imagine that it would be left to the discretion of the buyer as to whether they would develop and perhaps publish the pictures or simply keep the camera and film intact as an art piece in itself.

Introduce a system in which motorists are billed annually for any recorded traffic violations. Drivers who do not incur any penalties for parking, speeding or such like within a 12-month period would be refunded their road tax. The aim of the scheme would be to provide free motoring for law abiding drivers, funded in full by those who break the rules.

Rupert Kaye
22 August 2000

Found an agency representing female builders, plumbers, decorators and such like. In addition to pooling the resources of all existing women in the trades, the company would encourage others to enter into these professions. The attraction for the public would be clear: women are perceived as more trustworthy, considerate and generally agreeable.

Becky Clarke
23 August 2000

Design a photographical Internet search engine. The homepage of the engine would present a view of the earth from space that could be rotated using the mouse. Right-clicking would enable the viewer to progressively zoom in on continents, countries, places and, finally, specific buildings. A left-click at any point (on a cloud, a building, even a single shop or model of car) would call up websites best matching or supporting the object focused upon.

Chas Bayfield
24 August 2000

Produce a range of household paints and soft furnishings based on the colour palettes employed in famous works of art. The brochure would show, for example, Monet's 'Water Lilies' with colour swabs and an illustration of the colours working together in a living room with carpet, walls, cushions and curtains all combining to beautiful effect.

David Owen
25 August 2000

Editor's note:
This idea has now been put into practice in the UK by Virgin Trains. We have republished it here in the hope that the London Underground follows suit.

Install entertainment systems in underground and overground train carriages offering a variety of different radio channels (music, news, sport, listings) in a similar fashion to in-flight packages. Passengers would access the entertainment by plugging their own headphones into standard pins. The licence fees charged to operate each of the channels would be reinvested in running the underground and national rail services.

Justin Cooke
26 August 2000

Develop a virtual reality (VR) system for specific use with gym exercise machines. Rather than listening to music or watching MTV, exercisers could run through the streets of New York, row in an eight at the Olympics or cycle the Tour De France. All VR software and exercise machines in the gym would be synchronised allowing individuals to set times for themselves to improve or compete with others.

David Jones
27 August 2000

Build a replica of Noah's Ark to the actual biblical specifications. This modern recreation of an ancient maritime wonder would be 133m long, 22m wide and 13m high with three enormous decks housing museums of biblical and natural history and, on the top deck, restaurants, shops and a full-size movie theatre. The Ark would tell the amazing story of the earth's creation and development by juxtaposing theological and scientific accounts. The Ark would be a symbol of hope: encouraging responsible, sustainable and ethical economic development, and promoting the advancement of both human and animal rights.

Rupert Kaye
28 August 2000

Create a new brand of food and household products by simply adding the prefix 'The' before the name of the product. The Soap, The Tea and The Coffee would all be clearly defined products within an unlimited portfolio. The range would be sold in supermarkets but also in the company's own dedicated stores, 'The Shops'.

Chas Bayfield
29 August 2000

Editor's note:
Jay Pond-Jones really warmed to this one: 'You could create a franchise operation from this idea. It would be an easy way of unifying the nation's network of corner shops into a marketable organisation.'

Editor's note:
And to think that there were publishers who thought that 'The Big Idea Book' was a bit too quirky to find an audience!

13

Publish a book that can be read from both the front and the back. One half would be titled 'Old Tricks For New Dogs' and feature step-by-step line drawings of dogs being taught to fetch sticks, roll-over and play dead. The other half would be titled 'New Tricks For Old Dogs' and would feature dogs learning such tasks as online banking, text messaging and video conferencing. The latter half would be subtly targeted at people who may be too embarrassed to buy such a self-help book for themselves.

David Owen
30 August 2000

14

Produce a television show in which five applicants are selected and each given £1million. The lucky five must allow themselves to be filmed in a fly-on-the-wall style over the following 12 months. The show would chart the experiences of the newly made millionaires as they, their friends and family, come to terms with their good fortune.

Becky Clarke
31 August 2000

Introduce to customer service call-centres an option which allows callers held in a queue to push a button to have the call centre dial them back when they are next in line to speak with a representative.

Don! Snyder
1 September 2000

Editor's note:
This application is now a quite common feature of telephone hold systems but does anyone really trust the companies to call them back?

Produce designer plasters branded with the logos of companies such as Nike or Calvin Klein. These would not only sell to people with actual cuts and grazes but also to fashion victims.

David Owen
3 September 2000

Install sensors in parking spaces of multi-storey car parks such that a centralised system would know which spaces were unoccupied. Drivers entering the car park would be issued with a printed ticket displaying the position of the nearest available space. The system would offer an added advantage for drivers in providing a record of where their car is parked on their return.

Mark Waites
4 September 2000

Acquire detached residential properties and offer them for hire as venues for house parties. The houses would not sell alcohol and hosts or guests of each party would be responsible for providing their own food, drink and entertainment. However, cleaning services would be included in the hire fee. The hosts would be spared the stress of entertaining in their actual homes but as the houses would be fully furnished, guests would still enjoy all the trappings of a typical house party — bedrooms for the amorous, a garden for the talkers and the ubiquitous kitchen for those that are usually found there.

Chas Bayfield
5 September 2000

Develop a personal trainer service that is accessed by mobile phone. Exercisers would enter personal details such as height, weight, age, and so on into the website and choose from a selection of fitness plans. The system would then send reminders and targets each day or week by text message. The exerciser's phone would also function as a stopwatch during activities and could, with a fairly simple plug-in accessory, even take a pulse. 3G technologies would enable the duration of any activity to be relayed to the system, computed and the program adjusted accordingly.

Becky Clarke
6 September 2000

Design a range of study-aid bed linen. Sheets, pillowcases and duvet covers would be overprinted with exam revision notes including mind maps, mnemonics, quotations, diagrams and formulae enabling students to prepare for examinations in their natural habitat.

Rupert Kaye
7 September 2000

Editor's note:
At the time of publication, Rupert Kaye was a member of a think-tank established to highlight educational issues. We suspect that we got to publish this on the rebound – after the powers that be had given it short shrift.

Provide mobile phones for tourists to hire. In addition to offering typical pre-paid call services, the phones would be linked to an online resource of tourist information. All major destinations and attractions throughout the country would be supported by detailed information, which visitors could download to read or, with an earpiece, listen to as a tour commentary.

Steve James
10 September 2000

Produce mints for children called 'Sweet Teeth'. These would be small white mints fashioned in the shape of teeth. They would be sold in either mixed bags (incisors, molars, etc) or in more gimmicky sets of dentures. Children would be fascinated by the comic possibilities of placing mints under their pillow for the tooth fairy or spitting them out after mock accidents, while also being constantly reminded of the threat that sugar presents to their own teeth.

David Owen
11 September 2000

Open two restaurants: one called Tiffany's, which serves only breakfasts, and another called Just Desserts, which serves only desserts. Both ventures would share the same 24-hour premises, changing menus, staff, décor and signage at 3am and 4pm. The venue could offer special happy hours during the two changeover periods.

Chas Bayfield and David Owen
12 September 2000

Editor's note:
This was one of only a couple of ideas that genuinely had two authors. Chas Bayfield suggested Tiffany's and David Owen pitched Just Desserts. It was actually the novelty of the changeover between the two that earned the overall idea a place in this book.

Establish the Blue Chip Company to produce a range of alarmingly coloured food: blue chips, green cola, purple baked beans, etc. The unlikely colours would fascinate children, while their parents might better appreciate the pun.

Andy Evans
13 September 2000

Launch a radio station dedicated to broadcasting talking books. Programmes would be on the hour or half-hour to ensure listeners catch the start of any story or instalment. There would be regular slots devoted to particular genres of writing. Scheduling would feature chapters of children's titles in the evenings, the times for which would be staggered such that the reading ages corresponded to typical bedtimes. The station would be supported by the publishing industry who would supply previews of forthcoming releases, creating a similar relationship to the one that exists between music radio and record companies.

Becky Clarke
14 September 2000

Produce personalised passports for the Kingdom of God. Each passport would contain a photograph and an issue date. Instead of documenting countries visited, the passports could be stamped with rites of passage and points of spiritual growth and self-discovery. Suitable as Christening or Confirmation presents, these passports could also be given to a dying relative or friend as they prepare to travel to the hereafter.

Rupert Kaye
15 September 2000

Illustrate the dance routines of pop acts such as Steps or Janet Jackson on floor mats in a similar fashion to the numbered footprints used to learn ballroom dances. The mats could be made of thin plastic, folded and inserted into pop magazines such as Smash Hits.

Zoe Steventon
16 September 2000

Curate a web-based museum hosting an evolving collection of vintage website designs. The site might exhibit Amazon's launch design for example, or the first pages to incorporate Java or Flash technology, supported by comments from those involved in commissioning or designing the sites. The museum could also play host to examples of early spam or viral marketing.

Chas Bayfield
17 September 2000

Editor's note:
A whole street of neighbours might wish to work together and turn their road into a Wild West town or a tree-lined French boulevard, perhaps.

Allow homeowners to obscure their properties with hoardings more typically used by the construction industry. The board-fronted scaffolding could be decorated by an image chosen in preference to the frontage of the actual home (a country cottage or Georgian terrace, for example) or with advertising, which could fund actual redecoration.

Dan Friedman
18 September 2000

Compile an historical account of any given period by printing consecutive daily entries from a wide selection of published or unpublished diaries. The 1940s, for example, might be illustrated by an account of Churchill's day, followed by entries from individuals as diverse as Noel Coward, Anne Frank and Fred Perry. There could also be an appeal for extracts from diaries kept by members of the public during this period in order to present a truly varied record of the times.

David Owen
19 September 2000

Produce a range of scale-size, furry, cuddly mountains. These soft toy versions of, for example, The Eiger, Ben Nevis or Everest could be made from materials used by dedicated mountain-wear clothing lines such as Berghaus or North Face and carry their labels.

Alex Wilson-Smith
20 September 2000

Introduce a voluntary directory for mobile phone numbers. The directory could be accessed either online or on phones by text or mobile Internet, but not in published form. Individuals who wish to list their numbers could choose varying levels of security questions that would have to be correctly answered before the information was imparted. This would keep the numbers safe from telesales companies and help to establish the correct individual in the case of common names being searched.

Charlotte Savidge
21 September 2000

Editor's note:
When we started Idea A Day in the year 2000, mobile numbers were closely guarded and given out only to close friends or important business contacts. Now, it is home numbers that have become private lines.

Editor's note:
*Although the idea of
sponsoring a
cockroach or a rat
may not be as
instantly appealing as
contributing towards
the welfare of a
dolphin or tiger, it
would offer interesting
possibilities for those
wishing to give a
suitable parting gift to
a lecherous boss, a
squalid housemate or
an unfaithful lover.*

33

Establish a company called Rentoliv that would humanely capture and relocate pests rather than exterminate them. The company could offer adoption or sponsorship packages similar to initiatives undertaken by London Zoo and others.

Rupert Kaye
22 September 2000

34

Launch a web-based news service that would present the full history of current news stories. Most regular news broadcasts assume their audience has a knowledge of events leading up to the most recent developments but this is often not the case. The website would cover the origins of disputes in, for example, Northern Ireland or the Middle East on an international level, as well as offering background to specialised national or local stories.

Chas Bayfield
23 September 2000

Establish a business that offers services to living customers that would only be implemented after their death. The company would execute wills, maintain trusts or charitable donations, as well as undertaking more unusual services such as sending pre-prepared emails, birthday or Christmas greetings on behalf of the customer. Uniquely, the company would offer people a virtual afterlife as specialist staff would be trained to maintain correspondence with friends or companies in the style of the individual. A newspaper columnist, for example, could even continue to work and draw a salary after their death, with the new business and the deceased's estate splitting the income.

David Owen
24 September 2000

Editor's note:
The dead author Virginia Andrews publishes a new book every year, proving the point that the truth is stranger than even her psychotic fiction.

Manufacture LED display signs for use on the top or rear of cars that would be similar to those used by the police. Drivers could activate messages such as STOP or DANGER AHEAD from preset buttons on the dashboard. A voice-activated override would allow live streaming, which would be a great aid to motorists in convoy. The technology may also inspire a new craze for bumper stickers — only this time around, witticisms such as 'Babe on Board' or 'Not Daddy's Car' could be improvised.

Bill Bungay
25 September 2000

Open a boutique selling its own unique cocktails of goods such as sweets, crisps or even cigarettes. A box of cereal, for example, may contain an assortment of Cornflakes, Rice Crispies and Alpen in equal measures. The store's compounded products would be packaged and branded with a design visually representing the pick and mix theme and sold at a premium.

Dan Friedman
26 September 2000

Survey pedestrians passing through public areas for their postal or zip codes in order to derive a rate card by which advertisers and those providing field/sampling teams can be charged. The rate card would be used to establish a market for public spaces enabling train stations, airports and malls to accurately determine the value of the pedestrian flows they currently have. The research would also allow advertisers to negotiate better rates for display advertising, as their potential audience would be more clearly determined in advance.

John Griffiths
29 September 2000

Produce a docu-soap about a television production company making a docu-soap. Such a programme would offer the audience an opportunity to see how editorial decisions are taken, what was staged or what was left out, as well as the egos, rivalries and ambition that would most likely be even more evident in the production company than in their subjects. Both series, the show within the show and the show itself, would be broadcast together to further expose the truth of reality television.

David Owen
1 October 2000

Editor's note:
Rupert Kaye had an idea for a fly on the wall documentary about a fly on the wall. The idea was rejected but still, as this note proves, not forgotten.

Open an historically-themed food court offering cuisine from pre-existing cultures. Diners would be able to sample snacks and meals once popular with the Incas, Aztecs, Greeks, Romans or Vikings. The restaurant's educational benefits would attract school parties and history students while the novelty value of the project could be enhanced by themed décor and costumes.

Rupert Kaye
2 October 2000

41

Open a chain of food stores called Sell By Today, which would offer food items for sale only on their sell-by date. The store would buy in products from the major supermarket chains on the day before the sell-by date at discounted rates, and offer further bargains to customers. The stores would be positioned to appeal to office workers able to shop for the evening ahead. The chain would also work with homeless charities to co-ordinate distribution of food not sold by closing time.

Chas Bayfield
3 October 2000

42

Introduce parking meters either on public roads or in car parks that can be accessed remotely by telephone. Each space would have its own pin number allowing the owner of the vehicle the opportunity to top up their allocated time by credit card payment or reverse billed SMS without returning to the vehicle.

Dan Friedman
4 October 2000

Editor's note:
This is, of course, just one small step towards traffic wardens being legally bound over to call or text motorists in advance of issuing a ticket in order to give them a chance to rescue their vehicles.

Allow voters in political elections to cast a vote *against* a candidate. Voters would still have only one vote but each 'against' vote would nullify a 'for' vote. This system would give voters who are disenchanted with party politics, and perhaps unlikely to vote at all, at least the chance to express their feelings about a party they really do not want to be in power.

Brad Sims
5 October 2000

Produce emergency gift-kits to be sold in stores or vending machines at train stations. The kits would comprise a small present or voucher, a card, a pen and a stamp. The card designs would be abstract and blank on the inside in order to be appropriate for many occasions and greetings.

Becky Clarke
6 October 2000

Editor's note:
*The City of London is
packed with Damien
Hirst artworks.
Arguably, the
gleaming lobbies of
the international
banks provide the
most appropriate of
settings to view many
of the more
commercially oriented
modern artists.*

Publish a guide to corporate art collections. The book would offer practical and legal advice on how best to access lobbies and boardrooms or view art from the pavement.

David Owen
7 October 2000

Design a simple dashboard meter to calculate the actual cost of motoring. Information such as the initial cost of the car, road tax, insurance, and servicing would be entered before use, along with the car's fuel economy and petrol costs (which need to be regularly updated). The meter would measure distances travelled and compute an accurate cost of any journey, thereby giving the driver a real comparison to alternatives offered by public transport and the backup to charge passengers petrol money with authority.

Peter A Bethell
8 October 2000

Introduce a mobile Internet calorie-counter. Users would detail everything they eat during the day by selecting from menus on their phone. A program running on a website would approximate the calories for any food consumed and return a cumulative total. At any point in the day a user could request the total calories remaining from their preset maximum target. As they will have been supplying the site with their exact diet for some time, the system will be able to suggest foods that could still be eaten that day that would help balance their diet.

Becky Clarke
9 October 2000

Editor's note:
This was one of quite a few ideas that were originally published as 'WAP' applications. We will probably be hitting the 'find/change' function again for the next edition of the book – looking to update all the 3G references.

Launch a company called White Cabs. The drivers of the white taxis would be unqualified and currently undertaking The Knowledge. White cabs would be cheaper than black cabs, but would only be economical for passengers who knew the route to their destination, which they would have to explain to the driver. Customers would benefit from cheaper fares and the drivers would benefit from earning a living whilst accelerating their learning. The drivers would quickly pick up on short cuts and tips that local passengers would pass on. Taxis would be sprayed black when the drivers graduated.

Jan Van Mesdag
11 October 2000

Create a website of blank pages for individuals to doodle on while talking on the telephone or taking meetings from their desks. Users would use the mouse to draw simple ballpoint pen style lines on the blank page. In addition to providing a paperless means of mental exercise, the site could also analyse the drawings. The analysis service could include a 'find me a friend' function, which could provide contacts of other users with similar patterns of behaviour.

Steve James
12 October 2000

Open a restaurant without a kitchen. Each table would offer a selection of takeaway menus and a telephone offering direct connections to any of the affiliated take-out restaurants. Groups of diners would be able to order from a variety of meals to suit individual tastes. Staff would be easy to hire as the only skills required would be serving drinks and clearing tables. The restaurant would earn income from selling drinks, commission from the participating takeaways and perhaps from a nominal entrance fee.

David Owen
13 October 2000

Introduce charitable public conveniences. These toilets would have a relatively high charge for entrance — £1, for example. Half of the entrance fee would be used to maintain a very high level of cleanliness and general upkeep while the other half would go to a specific charity. The scheme would improve the quality of public toilets. Benefiting charities could run an ad campaign for the loos using the strapline: 'Do you give a s**t about charity?'

Liam Donnelly
15 October 2000

Launch an email service that carries advertising in each sent message. The ads would appear at the end of the email in the form of a billboard-style poster or banner ad. The ad space would be sold to specific advertisers based on demographic information submitted by the owner of the account about both themselves and their regular correspondents. In return for signing up to the mail service, account holders would not only be offered free email but actually paid an annual fee for regular use.

Chas Bayfield
17 October 2000

Editor's note:
Advertising in email is now commonplace. Considering the publication date, Charles Cohen raised the possibility that Chas Bayfield might plausibly be able to lay claim to at least inspiring its uptake — not that that would make him particularly popular, of course.

Develop an intruder alarm for cars, homes and business premises that, in addition to triggering a ringing alarm, also calls or sends a message to the owner's mobile phone with specific details on which element of the circuit has been broken. The owner could then return to the property or call neighbours to check if there is an actual break in rather than a false alarm. The same service could also be applied for home smoke or gas alarms.

Dan Friedman
18 October 2000

Introduce a third brake light to vehicles as standard. This light would be positioned in the rear window or boot lid of cars, as is quite common in recent designs, but would be made up of a sequence of bulbs. The degree of braking would be indicated by the number of illuminated lights. This will allow the driver behind the vehicle a better understanding of the first driver's intentions, aiding the flow of heavy traffic and preventing accidents caused by unnecessarily heavy braking.

Ian Walls
19 October 2000

Establish an official Martian Government, which would initially be based on earth. The government would be genuinely responsible for affairs on Mars such as planetary exploration, settlement and commerce. As an internationally coordinated project, the Martian Government would also serve as a research and development tool for experimental political systems and models of government that may later be employed on earth to represent whole continents or, ultimately, the whole planet.

Rupert Kaye
20 October 2000

Editor's note:
British Euro-sceptics might argue that such an alien government has been running in Brussels for some years already.

Open a supermarket selling only brand names and only the top brand name in each product sector. The same shelf space normally employed to display a range of competing brands would be filled with just one product. There would be fridges filled with Coke and whole aisles of Heinz beans. Shoppers could vote for the leading brands in each sector and food companies would compete for the status of being selected. The store would cultivate a brand-name culture, inspiring top-brand cookbooks or themed brand-name-only dinner parties.

David Owen
21 October 2000

Editor's note:
If successful, the proprietors might well expect their feature products to be supplied free of charge by the grateful manufacturer.

57

Employ the energy expended on exercise equipment in gyms to power the gyms themselves. Cycling, rowing and other equipment could be connected to dynamos and a generator, producing enough power to provide electricity throughout the complex.

Revd. Graham Peacock
23 October 2000

58

Develop software that allows users to customise generic literature such as romantic novels. Mills & Boon would be the perfect partner in a website hosting the service. Users would enter the names of friends as characters and base the stories in places and scenarios common to their own lives. Customers could download a digital version of the novel or, for a premium price, order a published version complete with artwork, which would make a unique gift. Mills & Boon would have an option to publish results which proved to be particularly successful.

Becky Clarke
26 October 2000

Encourage the world's mail services to provide free mailing to and on behalf of any registered charitable organisation. To avoid fraud, the charities would include their charity number as a line of their address, which could be crosschecked with the charity's name on a database.

Jim Bolton
27 October 2000

Install vending machines at underground, rail and bus stations to dispense vitamins. The machines would be similar in appearance to those that typically hold nuts, jellybeans or other confectionery. The availability of vitamins at stations would appeal to commuters who forget to take their daily doses. Tablets would probably cost about 10p each. Vitamins and pills on offer could change seasonally to include zinc in the winter or hay fever remedies in the summer. The government could even utilise the machines during epidemic outbreaks.

Justin Cooke
28 October 2000

Editor's note:
The fact that many breeds of dog are avid diggers would also dispense with the need to carry around a spade.

Design a metal detector to be worn by dogs. The device would strap around the underbelly of the dog. With a particularly enthusiastic animal straining at the leash, the physical effect would not be dissimilar to wielding an actual metal detector, although, with the dog off the lead and with the owner listening remotely with headphones a lot more ground could be covered.

Dan Friedman
29 October 2000

Create a secure online site where users can enter personal information of the sort required by credit card companies on application. The site would then determine the user's credit standing and select the most competitive card, focusing on special introductory offers. The user would empower the site to switch accounts whenever the best available offer was beaten by another card. Ultimately, the site would aim to offer customers a single credit card on which purchases or advances would be charged against the best account currently held. The site would combine bills from the multiple accounts and the user need only make one payment against their combined balance.

James Cramer
30 October 2000

63

Open a gift shop that sells time. Many people have quite enough things cluttering their houses and don't necessarily want any more. The shop would sell time as gifts – a day paint-balling, a night at the theatre, two hours with an interior designer or even an hour's ironing undertaken by someone else.

John Griffiths
31 October 2000

64

Establish a music library for motorists. Tapes and CDs would be available at petrol stations across the country. Music could be borrowed from one outlet and returned or exchanged at another.

Sergei Ivanov
1 November 2000

Editor's note:
One would expect to lose a fair number of tapes and CDs under this scheme but if, after registration and the loan of the first CD, further CDs were only lent in receipt of the first, the loss rate could be contained. This idea could go a long way to differentiate one petrol chain from its competitors.

Editor's note:

If, in addition to the real time serialisation, the extracts were published in geographically appropriate papers (Warhol in New York, Orton in London) readers would not only get a unique insight into the writers' lives over a period of time but could also visit the same locations on the same days, potentially meeting other readers.

Serialise classic published diaries such as those by Joe Orton, Andy Warhol or Anne Frank in daily newspapers. The dates of publication should correspond to the date of writing. If the diarist did not make entries for certain days then there would be no publication. The changes in the season and the impact of certain annual events would possibly bring the reader to a much more empathetic appreciation of the diarist's day-to-day life.

David Owen
2 November 2000

Introduce a ratings system for churches. Churches would be evaluated on the sincerity of the worship offered; the warmth of welcome visitors could expect; the church's active involvement in the local society; crèche facilities and such like. The most dynamic and hospitable places of worship would then be entitled to display their 'five cross' rating outside for all to see — thus assisting the spiritually curious, or Christians new to an area, in their choice of church. A detailed 'Which Church?' report could be published annually.

Revd. Graham Peacock
3 November 2000

Design a range of T-shirts which, on a first impression, declare the wearer to be a big fan of The USA, Phil Collins, Chelsea FC or whatever is declared on the shirt. This name or entity would be printed in large letters but below it in much smaller lettering would be a contradictory message such that an example might read: OASIS — I'm not a big fan. The shirts would allow brave or perverse individuals to enjoy the ridicule or misplaced appreciation of others but then, on closer inspection, to shatter their illusions.

Jim Bolton
4 November 2000

Establish an online appointment system for doctors, dentists, veterinary surgeons and other practitioners. The site would offer patients access to appointment books to view available time slots. A preliminary questionnaire could be used to prioritise urgent cases and brief doctors in advance of seeing the patient. In some cases doctors could advise patients by phone or email where an actual appointment would not be necessary. The system could be centrally maintained and franchised to local practices.

Glennette M. Clark
8 November 2000

Scour the book-publishing trade press for announcements of new autobiography commissions. When suitable subjects were found, individuals could attempt, without endangering or stalking the subject to secure a mention in the forthcoming memoir. Approaches may include dating the subject's children, crashing cars outside their homes or falling from a hot air balloon into their gardens. Following a series of successful publications, individuals could write their own biographies; describing their efforts, examining their motives, and reflecting on the nature of celebrity.

Dan Friedman
9 November 2000

Editor's note:
A similar store could open in Los Angeles in which any items that have been purchased and used by Hollywood stars would be sold under one roof.

Open a store stocking only those 2000 or so products endorsed by the Royal Family. Called 'By Royal Appointment', the potential chain would be based at a flagship shop situated in central London and would no doubt be a top destination for many tourists.

David Owen
10 November 2000

Introduce Pizza Cheese, a foodstuff similar in principle to the cheeses containing nuts or fruit that are currently available. Pizza Cheese would offer a blend of all the ingredients of a pizza topping. One example might be mozzarella with tomato, pepperoni and mushrooms. The cheese could be cooked on pizza bases or bread to create an instant snack.

Paul Douglas
11 November 2000

Launch a language school that also functions as a dating agency. Called the International Language of Love, the school would pair up couples who have common interests, a mutual attraction and a complementary desire to learn each other's language.

Sergei Ivanov
13 November 2000

Editor's note:
Despite being more cheesey than idea 71, this will always be a favourite. It could bring a little of the spirit of holiday romances to everyday life in the city.

Design a personal stereo that could produce a signal that can be shared by multiple users via remote headphones. The revenue for the manufacturer would be chiefly derived from sales of additional headsets as the opportunities for noise-free parties or even passive musical eavesdropping on trains is fully realised by the public.

Alex Wilson-Smith
14 November 2000

Editor's note:
Horseshoe shaped knee pads and gloves might also be provided for the parents.

Design a riding saddle for young children to ride on the backs of adults. The saddle, complete with reins and stirrups, would improve the safety of a popular toddler entertainment and act as a perfect introduction to horse riding proper.

Angela Hill
15 November 2000

Rebuild and restore all seven Wonders of the Ancient World in, or as close as possible to, their original locations. The project may provide welcome relief to the countries within which the wonders were situated, as they would benefit from increased tourism (particularly welcome to Iraq with regard to the Hanging Gardens of Babylon).

Rupert Kaye
17 November 2000

Publish an average national-rate card for services provided by plumbers, car mechanics, decorators, builders and so on. Customers would be able to reference the rate card online to verify that they have been quoted reasonable prices and aid them in negotiations.

Sarah Forrest
18 November 2000

Editor's note:
An average national price list for all goods from a pint of milk to a family estate car could also be of value. It would allow retailers to demonstrate the value of competitively priced goods and raise awareness amongst customers as to when they are overpaying.

Publish further chapters to supplement the Christian Bible. A 'third testament' could be edited by respected Christian leaders from any denomination who would be elected as guest editors on an annual basis. They would solicit submissions from all Christians wishing to contribute stories of their spiritual life.

Charles Addison
19 November 2000

Introduce a back up system for mobile phone address-books, call histories and other stored data. Users would be provided with a number to call in order to upload data to a central server, something they could do as often as they saw fit. In the event of losing the handset all saved information could be downloaded to the replacement phone and SIM card.

Dan Friedman
20 November 2000

Launch a language-translation phone line for international travellers. The traveller would carry one internationally recognised number specific to their native language and the call centre would route their call through to the appropriate translator. Callers would explain what they wanted to say before repeating the translated phrases or handing the phone over to the shop assistant, taxi driver or policeman.

Steve Sargent
21 November 2000

Introduce a premium rate phone-line service to be manned 24 hours a day by company personnel who would consider any question and simply answer with a 'Yes', 'No' or 'Please rephrase the question' to the best of their ability and knowledge. Anyone could call the line and ask anything they liked. Although it is possible that politicians and chairs of major companies might call, the service would most likely appeal as a novelty way to settle arguments or as a lifeline for desperate individuals in need of guidance but distrustful of telephone psychics.

David Owen
22 November 2000

Editor's note:
A live translation service for telephone calls might also prove popular. It would be no more complicated than a multi-lingual call-centre operator sitting in on a conference call. The idea need not be limited to the translation of foreign languages – grandparents could use the service to communicate with their rather more streetwise and slang-happy grandchildren, perhaps.

Editor's note:
*Steve James also
made claims for a
giant blanket of
optical fibres that
could render a tank
invisible. We thought
we'd run this more
modest, although
equally improbable,
application of the idea
and see if anyone
raised any scientific
objections.*

81

Design a cloak of invisibility by fabricating a garment from optical fibres. The fibres would be carefully arranged such that the ends of each fibre would be positioned on opposing sides of the body when worn.

Steve James
23 November 2000

82

Develop an online service, called mybartab.com perhaps, which would allow users to pre-purchase bar tabs for pubs, bars and clubs. The facility could serve a number of purposes such as imposing limits on a group or individual's drinking for an evening or enabling either cash or credit card-free nights out. Perhaps the most likely or useful application of the site would be in creating a new form of gift — a generous tab at a venue of choice would be a novel and almost effortless present.

Josh Carrico
24 November 2000

Manufacture The Iron Man, an inflatable torso of heat-proof latex that would make ironing shirts and tops an effortless process. The torso would emit steam via thousands of pinholes, which would smooth out creases in the garments. The size of torso would also be set by steam pressure such that one size fits all.

Martin Read
29 November 2000

Open a chain of Monopoly cafés in London. The cafés would not be overly accessorised with features from the board game but would simply be located on each street or station featured in the game and colour coded accordingly.

Chas Bayfield
27 November 2000

Editor's note:
The chain would maintain a competitive edge in the café market due to the fact that customers would always know where to find them. Friends could confidently arrange to meet at the Monopoly Café in Old Kent Road or at Fenchurch Street Station, without ever having been there before.

Design domestic radiators that can fold out from the wall to function as heated clothes dryers.

Becky Clarke
26 November 2000

Editor's note:
This idea would require a regular change of hosts. The interviewer may know nothing in the first broadcasts but after four or five weeks, Britney Spears would say that she was a pop singer and the host would say, 'Oh, maybe you know my friend Beyoncé!'

Produce a television chat-show featuring a host who would know absolutely nothing about their very famous guests. The host might, for example, be a Tibetan monk or African tribesman. Their questions — opening with 'Who are you?' — may reveal fundamental truths about the celebrity that are left undiscovered by the typically superficial and purely promotional chat-show appearances, while also providing a rich source of unintentional humour.

David Owen
1 December 2000

Create an Internet prison. This single page URL would be designed to appear like the interior of a prison cell. Companies and webmasters could embed a link to the URL in their sites. If visitors to the sites abused the services provided (by typing recognised swear words into an open message board, for example), they could be automatically redirected to the prison cell. Shareware code could be provided for webmasters to customise their own reprimanding message, which would be displayed by way of explanation to those detained.

Dan Friedman
3 December 2000

Develop a digital radio service for car stereos that would use GPS technology to stream spoken-word tour guides to accompany a journey. The service would be available primarily to accompany road trips through areas of scenic or historic interest and could be advertised on roadside signs. The discussion of points of interest would be synchronised to average speeds on the roads in question.

Lucille Kaye
4 December 2000

Editor's note:
Or, in a slightly more practical variation, audio guides to popular rail journeys could be provided to passengers on CD – anyone having to pause the commentary for more than an hour could claim a refund.

Launch a chain of personal-shopping consultants located on the high street or within shopping centres, who would provide measurement and recommendation services to people shopping for clothes. The consultants would be able to access a complete inventory of all current stock and prices in each local outlet but would not be directly associated with any particular store. Shoppers would make an appointment and pay for the service. Following the consultation, they would receive a list of suitable items that could be reserved for them in advance.

Becky Clarke
6 December 2000

Design a vacuum cleaner that the user straps onto their back to clean the home. The backpack deportment would allow greater freedom of movement and be particularly useful on stairs.

Greg Field
7 December 2000

Introduce postage stamps carrying a prominent advertisement or corporate logo as part of their design. These postage stamps would be sold at a discounted rate to the public, which the advertising and sponsorship revenue would underwrite. In addition to cost savings, many republicans would be only too happy to send materials without the need to stick a picture of a monarch's head on each and every envelope they mail.

Rupert Kaye
8 December 2000

Launch a web-based restaurant guide offering users the ability to search the menus of participating restaurants for particular dishes. Submitting 'Sticky Toffee Pudding' to the search engine would result in a list of restaurants ordered by locale and price. The site would be linked to an established review guide in order to qualify the results. Participating restaurants would be provided with an interface to submit daily menus and specials.

David Owen
9 December 2000

Establish an online directory of dormant websites. These sites would either have been found by the search engine as unchanged for a period of 12 months, or submitted by the owners following a decision not to continue with a project. Visitors to the directory would be able to view dead websites and, should they find a site they wish to resurrect, bid for it online.

James Cragg
12 December 2000

Editor's note: This idea offers a particularly clear picture of its inspiration and you can be sure that it was Dan Friedman rather than his partner who was woken unnecessarily early every weekday morning.

Develop personal alarms that would wake people by means other than sound. These devices might be designed as bracelets that constrict, vibrate or even inject the wearer. The alarms would allow couples with different work schedules to get up without waking each other up at the same time. They could also be employed by anyone who needs to sleep covertly — office staff in the habit of snoozing at work, for example.

Dan Friedman
13 December 2000

Establish an international forum on animal welfare along the lines of Amnesty International and under the name Animal International. The basic minimum rights that animals can expect would be drawn up, based on certain categories such as pets, farm, wild, working, zoo, circus and so on. The worst animal-rights abuses would be exposed and members would be encouraged to petition governments and the perpetrators of the abuse peacefully by letter.

Chas Bayfield
14 December 2000

Manufacture programmable neckties. Powered by a tiny rechargeable battery, each tie would actually consist of an LCD and a programmable memory capable of storing hundreds of designs from the sublime to the ridiculous.

Rupert Kaye
15 December 2000

Design an LCD window. This window would allow sunlight to pass through at one setting but also block out all light by simply adjusting the polarity of the LCD. The device would also allow the owner to display a customised window scene to be viewed from the inside, or a message to be viewed externally by hooking up the window to a computer.

Will Nickson
16 December 2000

Editor's note:
Jay Pond-Jones pitched this idea to a well-known confectionary brand with a spectacular punning title for the project. Now, you can play the ad man. What product was it? And what was the pun?

Launch a millionaire fund on the Internet created by one million individuals each donating one pound via credit card or online banking transfer. When the fund is complete, a millionaire entity will have been created. For each of the pound shareholders, this may be the closest they will get to being a real millionaire. Their pound will allow them a single vote in deciding how to collectively spend the money. An automated software programme will run presenting options for employing the fund, such as charity, investment or gambling. The range options would be available to the individuals to view in advance of their pledge.

David Owen
17 December 2000

Launch a digital television channel for the deaf. The channel would be based in the UK but available worldwide. As sign language is for the most part a global language, the UK production team would produce programming that would be especially welcome in countries where local programming for the deaf is poor or nonexistent. The collective international audience should be great enough to underwrite a commercial enterprise.

Ilana Glucksman-Thomas
18 December 2000

Introduce a premium rate phone-line service for motorists to call local taxi drivers and receive directions and advice before or during a journey. Drivers placing a call to the service would go through a switchboard and be connected to a cab driver who was not currently working a fare. Under the scheme, the drivers would receive payment for their time on the phone, neatly making up for time idled away at taxi ranks.

Angela Hill
19 December 2000

Editor's note:
Whether it is this idea that takes off or any of the other similar concepts in this book (phone a stranger, football-fan commentators or premium-rate landlines), this brand of one-to-one micro-business is sure to emerge if telecommunications services are deregulated further.

Conduct a survey of all national weather reports offered in print, on television and online. The reports would be tested for accuracy on a continual basis and the results published daily alongside a monthly top ten forecaster league. Through the report the public woud be able to place greater trust in the most accurate service based on their recent form.

Chas Bayfield
20 December 2000

Launch a marketing campaign for the board game Monopoly based around a competition offering genuinely free parking for life in central London or other cities featured in international versions of the game. The competition could be open only to purchasers of the game during the Christmas period. Such competitions could be held annually and offer houses on the Old Kent Road or in Mayfair as prizes and even free legal representation inspired by the 'Get Out Of Jail Free' card.

Dan Friedman
21 December 2000

103

Introduce video cameras into operating theatres such that patients under sedation or general anaesthetic could replay their operation after the event if they so desired. Quite possibly, such surveillance could be made a legal right of the patient and its primary application would be in ensuring that doctors and medical staff treat their patients with due respect. The tapes could also be used as evidence in malpractice lawsuits. The medical profession may be able to recoup some or all of the set up costs by selling videos to the kind of patient that would consider a tape an apt memento of their surgery.

David Owen
23 December 2000

104

Produce a television show called Ménage À Trois in which members of the public volunteer to share a three-in-a-bed sexual experience with two other participants unknown to them before filming. The individuals would be interviewed before the event and asked what they hope, or expect, from the experience (chiefly, what sex they would like their partners to be). The threesomes would then be randomly determined. No action would be shown on screen but the participants would be interviewed individually following their experience and then together in *Blind Date* style.

Sam Torme
27 December 2000

Editor's note: There are two questions we often ask when considering an idea for publication: Would this be popular? Would this offend? As this idea shows, a double 'yes' does not necessarily guarantee rejection.

105

Establish a Santa Claus telephone hotline. The seasonal service would allow children to talk on the phone to white-bearded, red-suited actors at a premium rate. Children would be encouraged to detail their Christmas wish lists and the recordings would later be phoned back to the caller number for the parents to jot down or transcribed on the Internet for access by extended family.

Rupert Kaye
28 December 2000

106

Introduce a tailoring service to clone individual items of clothing. Customers with well-loved but well-worn garments that are no longer available to purchase could pay a premium to have them copied as closely as possible. In addition to exact copying, a service would also be offered to modify items with regard to size, colour or cut.

Ben Nicholson
29 December 2000

102

Design a clothing range with unique code numbers attributed to each item. The purchaser or recipient of such a garment could use the PIN to access a website and chat room along with anyone else who has the same item of clothing. The opportunity would be presented to customers to share personal details and perhaps make friends with anyone with similar taste. Parties could possibly be organised by groups of people all dressed in the same clothes.

Sergei Ivanov
30 December 2000

Editor's note:
An idea of genuine social innovation but one that should never be crossed with blind-dating soirees. Having 40 people saying that they'll be the one at the bar in the red polo-neck jumper could be disastrous.

103

Launch a range of medicinal canned drinks. Any medicine that is usually sold in tablet or powdered form could be repackaged as dissolved drink. Canned morning after products such as Resolve, Alka Seltzer or Andrews would be ideal for hectic modern living and could even be sold in clubs for consumption on the night bus home.

Becky Clarke
1 January 2001

109

Launch a website called bannerad.com, which would provide an archive of every banner ad posted on the Internet. The site would be developed initially as a resource for business and academic reference. However, once the site had generated a sufficient number of visitors, advertisers would be charged for banner placement, thereby completing the revenue circle.

Nishin Manko
2 January 2001

110

Editor's note:
Trevor Webb, winner of the 2002 Idea of the Year award, is the only person who has not only had every idea he has submitted published on the site, but every one of them has made it into the book.

Create an arcade videogame based around an underwater scuba diving adventure. An actual aqualung would be attached to the games console. Players of the game would start with a two-minute air supply and would need to find certain objects or kill opponents to release more oxygen. A sensor in the mouthpiece would ensure that the player breathes only through the snorkel. When the air runs out, the player would have to remove the mouthpiece and the game would be over.

Trevor Webb
3 January 2001

Introduce 'Autobarns', a chain of garage spaces situated on the outskirts of cities that would provide ramps, equipment, tools and access to spare parts for motorists keen to undertake their own repairs and servicing. Use of the Autobarns would be charged hourly and could include consultation from expert mechanics. Should any individuals be unable to repair their own car, a full service and on site garage could take on the work.

Chas Bayfield
5 January 2001

Produce a range of stickers with bright colours, pretty patterns, photographs and amusing phrases on them to fit the size of government health warnings on consumable products such as cigarette packets. Regular users of the products, who are perfectly aware of the harm that the product is doing to their health, could then put a positive spin on their chosen course of action.

Justin Cooke
6 January 2001

113

Editor's note:
In the event of serious delay, passengers could be refunded instantly by paying less or nothing at all, rather than waiting for a claim to be processed.

Introduce a deferred payment system for airline tickets such that passengers pay only on arrival at their destination. The airlines would swipe passengers' credit cards on departure but only charge them when they disembark. Although saving on the cost of a flight would offer scant compensation following a fatal crash, the system might further encourage airline safety.

Mark Waites
9 January 2001

114

Produce a television special introducing a new impressionist. Major celebrities would be secretly invited to overdub the mimic's attempts with their actual voices thereby creating the illusion of astonishing talent in an unknown individual. At some point after the broadcast, the hoax would be exposed but, as it will have been well-loved celebrities who have tricked the public, the show might well be forgiven and could even continue into a series.

Sam Torme
10 January 2001

Establish an online service to rate business cards. Each card submitted would be scored out of 100 for design, delivery of information and status of the holder. Anyone could scan and submit either their own or someone else's card for rating by the independent panel. Cards would only be scored once and a copy saved on the site. Members of the business community could then collect, swap or trade cards in a fashion emulating the classic 'Top Trumps' card games. Individuals may even wish to reprint highly rated cards to display their high scores.

David Owen
11 January 2001

Develop mobile phone ring tones that mimic ambient or white noise. Typical office-based or urban sounds, such as the opening of a can of Coke, keys being struck by a typist or passing traffic, would be sampled and deployed as personal tones. The mobile user would train themselves to take notice of their own chosen sound, while others working around them would be less likely to be distracted.

Justin Cooke
14 January 2001

117

Introduce road signs sponsored by a leading map or road atlas publisher, which would announce to motorists, 'You are leaving page 58. Please turn to page 64'. The signs would function both as advertising for the company and as a genuine reference for travellers.

Chas Bayfield
17 January 2001

118

Design a range of fake fur coats that have all the comfort and style typically associated with such luxury garments but do not attempt to look like real fur. Fashion labels could, for example, develop a spotted fake fur with the spots vaguely in the shape of the company's logo.

Nick Clarke
18 January 2001

Establish a telephone number for members of the public who might be in some distress but unsure whether their predicament warrants the attentions of the emergency services. An 888 line would be introduced to relieve pressure on 999. Commonsensical volunteers able to offer simple advice and solutions would staff the service. When necessary, the staff would provide numbers for local police stations or forward callers to the emergency services.

Kate Pirouet
19 January 2001

Editor's note:
About a year after this idea's original publication date, The Mirror reported that Suffolk police were to trail an 888 number, which was to work in just the same way. We can only assume that the trial was less than a rave success.

Establish a premium rate phone-line service to help individuals locate lost items such as keys or remember telephone numbers, street or web addresses. The service would be built around a questionnaire provided by a psychologist. Questions would range from the classic 'Where were you when you last remember having your keys?' to such subjective approaches as, 'What did you feel when you last looked at the website?' A unique system of billing could be employed whereby the call costs, say, £2 to place and becomes progressively cheaper the longer it takes.

David Owen
20 January 2001

Develop software for mobile telephones that once activated irreversibly dials a user's parents or grandparents on their birthdays and at regular intervals agreed by the user upon registration. The phone would place the compulsory call immediately after another call had ended to ensure that the user was available to talk. The owner of the phone would not be able to hang up, either when the phone was ringing or during the subsequent conversation. Only the grandparent or parent would be able to end the call.

Dan Friedman
21 January 2001

Offer an in-flight television channel relaying the view outside the aeroplane for travellers unable to secure a window seat.

Chas Bayfield
22 January 2001

Install an electronic display into nightclubs to publish the name of the track currently being mixed by the DJ. A tickertape machine could also constantly feed out the play list, allowing dancers to tear off strips and recall favourite tracks the next day.

Justin Cooke
24 January 2001

Editor's note:
This idea was superseded by the actual introduction of Shazam, the mobile service that identifies music being played. We could not be more envious of the Shazam founders — not just for thinking of such a perfect idea but for actually implementing it.

Introduce a personalised weekend-newspaper service allowing customers to order only the sections from the weekend papers that they actually want. The customer may request the business sections from all the Sunday broadsheets with the TV guide from a tabloid. A premium would be paid, certainly covering the cost of each newspaper from which they require sections. The newsagent may find, however, that in addition to attracting new customers that they would also make a greater profit from supplying multiple customers with opposing tastes and interests.

Brian Blair
25 January 2001

125

Broadcast commercials for a cleaning brand such as 'Mr Muscle' that look like typical adverts but actually have static dirt and fingerprints laid over the images. The audience may intuitively feel that the television could do with a polish, thereby making them a little more receptive to the product on offer.

David Owen
26 January 2001

126

Launch a yellow-hued shaving foam for smokers and coffee drinkers. No longer would devotees of these two substances be alarmed by the sight of their stained teeth lurking behind a foreground of ice-white shaving foam.

Davey Moore
28 January 2001

127

Appropriate the skills and training of sniffer dogs for domestic use. Anyone who has lost something could contact the dog and a handler directly from any public directory. A briefing would involve presenting other personal items to the dog and outlining the area of loss to the handler.

Mark Chalmers
29 January 2001

128

Open a shop in an area of great wealth, such as Monaco, Beverly Hills or Dubai, that would open its doors only once a month and only to five customers. On display would be five numbered items worth between $100 and $1m. Each customer would sign an agreement and then pick a number corresponding to an item for sale and another number corresponding to a price ticket. The customers would gamble on buying a $1 artefact for $1m rather than the other way round. The store's mark up and profit would be guaranteed in any eventuality.

Dan Friedman
31 January 2001

Editor's note:
One would have to assume that the biro bought for $1m would be so famous an item that its value at auction would go some way to recouping the customer's loss.

129

Organise a pro-celebrity-resident golf tournament in a suburban cul-de-sac. A round would be played from one lawn or grass verge to another (over houses, ponds, swimming pools and greenhouses), with all other areas (roads or pavement) being out of bounds. Income from television rights would be shared among residents.

David Owen
2 February 2001

130

Invent an unobtrusive girdle that supports heavily pregnant women's abdomens. The device, similar in essence to a brassiere, would provide much needed support and help prevent the muscular pain and backache sometimes suffered during the third trimester.

Matthew Martell
3 February 2001

131

Launch a website offering topical T-shirt designs inspired by breaking news stories or emerging trends. The designs would be available for download in a format compatible with iron-on transfer paper stocks currently available. The site would also sell the transfer paper and batches of plain T-shirts.

Jonas Crabtree
5 February 2001

Editor's note:
It is the speed at which people could be wearing topical T-shirts that makes this idea so exciting. Football fans could be out at the pub with the half-time score in a big football match printed on their chests. It might only be the ironing that would stop this from becoming a phenomenon at football grounds.

132

Introduce a new factor to determine seat allocations on aeroplanes. In addition to requesting an aisle or window seat, passengers would declare their status as married, single or WLTM (Would Like To Meet). As a result of such seat planning, the flight time could be far more socially dynamic. It should also be noted that just as the system would engineer encounters, it could be also be employed to remove such distractions for the antisocial passenger.

Mark Chalmers
6 February 2001

133

Install a second horn in cars. The original horn would be used for hazard warnings or to communicate anger or outrage and would maintain a typically harsh sound. The second horn would be for thanking people, or saying goodbye when pulling away from friends. This horn would have a happier, more comic tone and be visually represented on the dashboard accordingly.

Lorna Bateson
7 February 2001

134

Create a 'Not the Boss' alert function for individuals involved with handling sensitive data in the workplace. If the individual felt that the data on their monitor was in jeopardy of being compromised, a simple click of the button would replace it with the home page of an irreverent site such as amihotornot.com, theonion.com or the like.

Justin Cooke
8 February 2001

135

Produce a DVD compilation of the all the goals scored against, rather than by, a particular team in a season or decade. The series would kick off with the commercial certainties provided (at least in the UK) by Germany, Argentina or Manchester United compilations.

David Owen
9 February 2001

136

Develop a Chastity Pill that would be effective for 12 to 48 hours. The pill, which would completely quell any sexual urges, would be force-fed to untrustworthy partners about to embark on a business trip or just out on the town with single friends.

Steve Sargent
10 February 2001

Editor's note:
This pill might also be used to ensure that first dates or social engagements with supposedly platonic friends of the opposite sex do not get out of hand.

137

Incorporate a recording function into the design of car stereos that would allow drivers to save a particular piece of music or information in a news bulletin that they might find useful at a later date. With digital radio, the files could be recorded and sent to the driver's computer, PDA or phone.

Inderjit Singh
11 February 2001

138

Launch a marketing campaign for a new novel by publishing the author's work in progress on the Internet. A simple interface would mirror the writer's word processing software live on the web. The online audience would see words and sentences appearing in real time. They would also see corrections being made and lines being deleted.

Sam Torme
12 February 2001

Launch a live digital-television channel on which a panel of experts discuss which television show people should be watching at that moment in time on any of the other available channels.

Chas Bayfield
13 February 2001

Editor's note:
This idea proved so popular during the editing of this book that a company was launched by certain members of our review committee to make it happen. Now a programme called Flipside.

Launch an umbrella-sharing scheme in a major city. Companies would be invited to sponsor the manufacture and distribution of thousands of umbrellas, which would carry their advertising. The public would be encouraged to take and deposit the umbrellas at public places, train stations, offices or restaurants as required.

David Owen
14 February 2001

Editor's note:
Useful as umberellas are, this idea would ease the frustrations of owning them on a permanent basis (ie. storing them when wet, losing them and carrying them when it's not actually raining).

141

Produce a novelty range of complete, miniaturised meals so that diners could, for example, eat a Sunday roast followed by Salmon en Croute with new potatoes and green beans, followed by a Mixed Grill, followed by a Chicken Tandoori with Pilau rice. Each meal would be a quarter the size of a normal meal but lovingly crafted as an exact scale replica.

Alex Wilson-Smith
15 February 2001

142

Editor's note:
The inclusion of radio stations on digital television is by no means an adequate swap for what we consider to be a far more valuable innovation.

Stream the audio track from television broadcasts as digital radio. Would-be viewers, stuck in the office, in traffic or even on holiday, could listen to their favourite shows via the Internet or in their cars. Audio-only snooker might prove less than exciting, but the soundtrack to a soap opera could well be sufficient to convey the storylines, and dropping the visuals might actually improve some shows.

Dan Friedman
16 February 2001

143

Provide retail therapy as a legitimate prescribed treatment. Retail therapy vouchers would be available to patients to the value of the drugs they would otherwise be taking and would be redeemable in high street shops. An agreement with retailers would enable larger goods to be returned if the patient recovered sufficiently.

Mark Chalmers
17 February 2001

144

Organise an unofficial online army on behalf of the United Nations. Any individual could join the cause and aid in the spreading of targeted viruses or hacking/crashing the computer systems of hostile powers.

Mary Slim
19 February 2001

Design photo-booths that, by means of audio-visual or physical prompts such as an electric shock, could elicit a range of poses and expressions in the subject. Customers would use the device to help create the look they require. If someone needed to supply a picture with a job application for a position in a crèche or nursing home for example, they could be photographed while enjoying images of puppies or kittens and listening to The Carpenters.

David Owen
20 February 2001

Editor's note:
It is also possible that university students could actually be working to solve genuine problems for companies willing to sponsor their education.

Allow for university examinations to be sponsored by major corporations and brands to help financially support students. A company such as Orange, for example, could pose questions in technology, sociology or English exam papers based on a future-related topic. The brightest answer might then be published as an advertisement for Orange in the national press.

Alex Wilson-Smith
21 February 2001

Create an on and offline loyalty exchange, where individuals can trade loyalty points from one scheme against others that they find more useful on a barter basis. The exchange would have in-built links to all loyalty-scheme operators, allowing individuals to maintain a personal overview of all their loyalty relationships, much as they do their financial ones. Online trading and associated values of particular loyalty points would also be a good indicator of brand strength.

Tim Kitchin
22 February 2001

Open an eat-as-much-as-you-like buffet restaurant that weighs diners when they enter and again when they leave. The restaurant would charge diners according to the amount of weight they have put on. It might also encourage healthy diets in regular customers who opt for lean meats, salads and soufflés to keep the bill as low as possible.

Tom Childs
23 February 2001

Editor's note:
The toilets would have to be even more heavily guarded than those at the McDonalds in Piccadilly Circus.

149

Remake a film that previously flopped at the box office with a stronger cast, tighter script, better director or higher effects budget and release the new version a year after the initial failure. Should the film still fail to find a mass audience, the process would be repeated on an annual basis. As one hit pays for many failures in the film business, the instant-remake plan would offer an attractive double-or-nothing financial model for a studio. The very novelty of the concept would ensure huge PR and word of mouth, and the annual releases could become cult events in their own right.

Dan Friedman
24 February 2001

150

Design a smart volume-control for personal stereos that would monitor ambient noise levels and adjust the playback volume accordingly. When on a train, for example, the volume would be higher when travelling at speed than when stationary.

Steve James
26 February 2001

Produce chocolates that look like computer keyboard keys. This geek food could be packaged in a box that looks very much like a laptop. Using an index inside the lid, the alphanumeric character printed on each key could indicate which flavours were which far more accurately than the shape outline system currently favoured.

Tristan Spill
27 February 2001

Editor's note:
Which leads us to wonder if an online guide to all known chocolate shapes and centres might not be such a crazy scheme in itself. Or better still, launch a company which invites the confused members of the public to send in rogue chocolates for the staff to take a bite, come to a conclusion and send the remainder back with a written report.

Build an arm-wrestling machine that could be attached to a tabletop and linked to the Internet via a computer. Players could challenge the machine on a range of settings but also wrestle anyone else in the world with the same machine. In two-player mode, the motorised arm would flex to measure one user's strength, and then map their force against the other competitor and respond accordingly.

Mary Slim
1 March 2001

Editor's note:
*Wayne Hemingway
read this and
suggested hopping on
a Qantas flight. It
would certainly be a
suitable joint venture
between UK and
Australian retailers.*

153

Launch a chain of shops selling a selection of out-of-season items of clothing from major high street stores — shorts and swimwear in the winter, hats and coats in the summer. The stores would offer retailers an alternative to discounting last season's stock and appeal to customers preparing for ski or winter sun holidays.

Mark Hampshire
2 March 2001

154

Introduce a 'People Bus' scheme to a town or city. Pedestrians who regularly chose to walk rather than use public transport would volunteer to act as 'buses'. The volunteers could carry GPS sets, wear 'People Bus' jackets or hats and would update a website via their mobile phones as to the journeys they were undertaking on foot. Citizens considering taking a walk could check the website or their phones for a 'People Bus' going their way and join them for company, security or guidance if they were unsure of the best route.

Steve James
3 March 2001

Introduce a lottery-style competition to public transport systems such as the underground to encourage general usage and reduce fare dodging. Each valid ticket passing through the electronic barriers on the tube, for example, would be considered as an entry to the lottery. If a passenger won a prize, the barrier would feed out a lucky ticket that could be immediately redeemed. Lucky tickets would be exchanged for incentive style prizes such as additional travel passes or credits at platform retailers.

Jim Richards
6 March 2001

Market business cards for children. The cards would feature the logos of football clubs, pop bands or TV shows, along with the bearer's name and, inevitably, their mobile phone number.

Chas Bayfield
7 March 2001

Editor's note:
We love the idea that kids could start swapping and trading each other rather than Pokemon. Five of the boy in the braces who always gets picked last for football for one Head Girl.

Open a retail outlet to sell goods that are out of date or circulation. Customers would be able to purchase The Sunday Times the following Friday or even a pre name-change Marathon bar from the freezer. Prices would increase the longer the items remained in stock. The shop would require considerable backing at the outset but could be relatively secure that when items sold, the profit margin would be sufficient to cover costs accrued during their shelf life.

David Owen
8 March 2001

Editor's note:
This idea was without doubt one of the all-time favourites on Idea A Day. Only fears over the creation of a Triffid/Dalek hybrid should stop this from happening.

Engineer solar-powered plant pots on wheels that would manoeuvre themselves around a patio as the sun moved around the sky. Each 'Ropot' would be programmed to seek out just enough sun and water to flourish. Quite uniquely, Ropot gardens would change in design throughout the day.

Steve James
12 March 2001

159

Release a series of audio recordings that play the sounds (or silence) of celebrities sleeping. These recordings could either be sold on CD or licensed to radio stations to fill night time schedules. Members of the public would be able to switch on the recordings as they go to bed and enjoy the experience of sleeping with their favourite personalities.

Trevor Webb
13 March 2001

Editor's note:
These CDs would not always be filed under Easy Listening. We would imagine that Lemmy, for example, probably snores with as much force and volume as his band rocks.

160

Produce a documentary series following the lives of a number of staunch smokers. The series would be filmed and broadcast in instalments over a number of years and would track the effects of the volunteers' habits. Annual updates would present full reports on their health, mental state and attitudes to smoking throughout their lives. The same format could be applied to subjects committed to drug or alcohol use.

Becky Clarke
14 March 2001

161

Allow mobile phone users to transfer credit to other 'pay as you go' users. Working in a similar fashion to reverse charge calls from payphones, the modification would be invaluable for rescuing friends left stranded without means or funds to activate their phones.

Aidan Corrigan
15 March 2001

162

Launch an online photographic library of genuine snapshot pictures. The company would offer the public a royalty on the commercial use of images submitted. High street labs such as Boots or Snappy Snaps could offer a simple tick box for customers who would like their film to be added automatically to the library. In addition to providing clients with a source of genuine images for commercial use, the library would operate as a research resource for anyone from historians to fashion designers.

David Owen
16 March 2001

Develop a studio-based television quiz show in which contestants are set very difficult questions to answer in real time and with no time limit. While thinking, the contestants would be pictured in a screen within the screen, while pop videos, cartoons, news features or adverts would be broadcast. Contestants would press a buzzer when they have an answer and be returned to full screen size.

Dan Friedman
17 March 2001

Design wrappers for individual tampons that can be used to dispose of a used tampon when a new one is opened.

Lucy Nicholls
18 March 2001

165

Curate an exhibition of contemporary photographic portraits where visitors to the gallery would become the subjects of the pictures. Whenever a visitor stopped to look at a portrait they would be photographed and their picture would replace the image they were looking at as soon as they moved away. Every viewer would then see a different and unique portrait, and by viewing it, create another.

Steve James
19 March 2001

166

Editor's note:
An almost completely unworkable and patently flawed concept for which we can offer no excuse whatsoever. Mary Slim must have been blinded by (Bluetooth) science. We were also sent an idea for a Bluetoothbrush, which was funnier but had no actual use whatsoever.

Design a domestic toaster that can burn letters and numerals onto slices of bread as they toast. Linked to the Internet by Bluetooth, the Toastwriter could print news headlines, football results or other such information. The machine could also allow for SMS or email messages to be sent by third parties. People separated from their loved ones could send text messages to appear as a surprise on their partner's toast.

Mary Slim
20 March 2001

167

Broadcast live footage from prisons on a pay-per-view basis. The footage could either be streamed from CCTV cameras or web cameras via the Internet. Paying viewers might range from the merely curious, to those fascinated by serial killers. Revenues could be used to lessen the dependence on taxpayers to pay for the prison service, while constant public monitoring might help ensure standards are met.

William Egleton
21 March 2001

168

Produce a collection of artworks based on well-known paintings or sculptures under the title 'Better Art'. Van Gogh's 'Sunflowers' would be revisited, for example, and the irregular shape of the vase corrected. While the success of, or need for, such improvements would spark some controversy, the poster series could offer kitsch appeal for the sophisticated art lover and welcome wall hangings for those who simply prefer the new versions.

David Owen
22 March 2001

169

Editor's note:
Anyone speeding would soon find their favorite artists singing in the style of Pinky and Perky. Whilst those wishing to use the reverse gear might uncover secret back-tracked messages.

Build roads with music or narrated information scratched into the surface. Cars would be fitted with a stylus and the recordings would play through the car stereo. These musical journeys could be employed to guide visitors around a large space such as a theme or safari park. For very wealthy homeowners, the technology could be employed to create unique driveways that greet visitors on their arrival.

Steve James
24 March 2001

170

Editor's note:
Clearly there is a chicken and egg problem here as the introduction of such barriers to any existing motorway would no doubt cause traffic chaos in either direction.

Engineer central barriers for motorways that can be moved to create more lanes in the direction of the greatest traffic flow.

Cassy Baker
25 March 2001

Promote retail sales online by offering heavily discounted goods for sale on a website but restricting the time each customer can spend browsing and purchasing to a couple of minutes. An individual visiting the site would be clocked-in, timed-out and refused entrance again for the duration of the online sale. The result would be similar to a trolley dash as customers sought to fill virtual baskets with bargains and complete credit card transactions before being locked out. Customers could earn extra time in the store by referring friends to the site.

Dan Friedman
27 March 2001

Manufacture tyres with fluorescent paint injected into them at the level of legal tread. Worn tyres would show in a different colour and be easily noticed by either the owner or the relevant authorities.

Scott Morris
28 March 2001

123

Editor's note:
*Surely, the world is a
better place just for
publishing this
thought. It certainly
adds a whole new
meaning to 'Protect
and Serve'.*

Empower police forces to cordon off areas of natural beauty or cultural significance rather than just accident or crime scenes. For example, an officer of the Metropolitan Police Force might wish to use some black and yellow tape to highlight and preserve a perfect patch of clover growing in Hyde Park.

Alex Wilson-Smith
30 March 2001

124

Editor's note:
*We are glad to note
that it is now possible
to buy Incredible Hulk
fists anf Nija Turtle
swords which do just
this.*

Design gloves for children that would make cartoon-like sounds when moved in a particular fashion. They might go 'Kaboom' when punched against a surface or person or make kung-fu sounds when moved violently through the air.

Tristan Spill
1 April 2001

Publish a coffee-table book of portrait photographs entitled KIOSK. Each page would present the face of one of the world's beautiful people; from fashion, music or film. The image would be selected from one of four taken in a passport-approved photo booth. No famous photographer. No make-up artist. No stylist. No airbrushing. The lighting would be solely that of the bulb in the booth. The model would be allowed one creative decision throughout the whole process — whether to have the kiosk curtain pulled behind them or not.

michaelsoft
3 April 2001

Launch a confessional telephone line. The confessions of anyone calling the number would be recorded and stored as a sound file on a server. In return for making a confession, users would be able to hear one of the other pre-recorded confessions at random.

Steve James
4 April 2001

Editor's note:
Of course, it might just be both apt and helpful for those who were truely contrite to choose instead a pre-recorded message of absolution. A word of forgiveness... or a sinful tale...

177

Erect digital billboards with which would the public could interact via mobile phones. Billboards advertising a television quiz show, for example, might display a question and a telephone number. If a passer-by called or sent a text with the correct answer, the billboard would be refreshed — crediting the individual and posting a new question.

David Owen
5 April 2001

178

Sell champagne in cans. The brand name would be Canpagne.

Peter Evans
6 April 2001

129

Launch a range of T-shirts featuring the faces of members of the public as designs. Each customer would send a passport photograph to the manufacturer. They would then be sent a shirt with a picture of someone else on it, but with the knowledge that the same person has a shirt displaying their face. A national pairs game could be introduced in which any two people that actually find each other and arrive together in their shirts at a designated place share a prize.

Sam Torme
9 April 2001

180

Launch a range of consumer financial-investment packages linked to weather conditions in a particular country or area. Poor weather would see an improvement in the fortunes of the portfolio and fine weather the reverse. Although the package would be designed to give a standard return over a period of years, the day-by-day fluctuation would help counteract the negative feelings felt by anyone who would typically feel despondent at the prospect of rain or grey skies.

Chas Bayfield
11 April 2001

181

Introduce kiosks to off-licenses enabling customers to design and print their own sticky labels for wine bottles. The off-licenses would offer unbranded bottles of house wines for customers to personalise as amusing gifts or talking points at dinner parties.

Becky Clarke
13 April 2001

182

Editor's note:
It was suggested that the cremation side of the business should simply be called 'Toast'.

Establish a funeral service promising to undertake burials or cremations as quickly and as cheaply as possible for those who really do not care for either ceremonies or the dead. If legally permissible, the company could offer to dispose of bodies within 24 hours of death.

Mary Slim
14 April 2001

183

Adapt the 'Who Wants To Be A Millionaire?' quiz format for domestic play in a micro-version entitled 'Who Wants Ten Quid?'. In pounds sterling, the first question would be worth 0.1p, and contestants would keep the money at 1p and 32p.

David Owen
15 April 2001

Editor's note:
We heard a fantastic report of a family who played this and the mother decided not to further risk the winnings she had accumulated. She walked away with £1.25.

184

Manufacture cycle locks with hollow tubes filled with compressed gas. As well as being considerably lighter than conventional locks, Gas Locks would be impossible for thieves to saw through and no more dangerous to carry around than a camping gas cylinder.

Alex Wilson-Smith
16 April 2001

185

Launch a web-based museum where the hard drives of famous or significant dead people would be available for posthumous inspection.

Chas Bayfield
17 April 2001

186

Editor's note:
If only there were a Nobel Prize for eccentricity. Steve James' obsession with making the world a better place through the most complicated of schemes demonstrates the most unique of talents.

Design a range of sunglasses called Respecs. The eyewear would have one lens polarized horizontally and the other vertically. Those viewing the world through the glasses would not really notice a great deal of difference to their outlook. It would however be impossible to make direct eye contact with other wearers of the same glasses, as the lens polarizations would cross, effectively blocking the line of sight. This event would act as an impromptu wink or secret acknowledgment between devotees of the glasses.

Steve James
18 April 2001

187

Introduce a service for customers wishing to subtly remind their friends of their own impending birthday. The service would send emails, text messages and even place phone calls to the targeted group of friends, dropping names and products or services associated with the customer into typical and unassuming conversation.

Dan Friedman
19 April 2001

188

Modify mobile phones to act as guns in a public but harmless war game. Handsets would be capable of locating other phones in the immediate vicinity. Mobile phone users would point and shoot, sending a signal to the target phone, which would send a text simply reading, 'You're dead'.

Sam Torme
20 April 2001

189

Editor's note:
*We wouldn't be at all
surprised if one the
primary uses of
mobile camera
phones was in
checking one's own
appearance.*

Modify mobile phone and PDA screens to act as mirrors. The backing of the display would be coated by a photosensitive material, which would appear reflective when an internal light was activated or an electric current passed through it.

Alex Pressland
21 April 2001

190

Editor's note:
*Jay Pond-Jones
reported that, 'I
suggested this very
same idea to a zoo
once. I also
suggested bringing in
a telecom partner to
fund it. They didn't
want to know. It's
frustrating this ideas
business.' Quite.*

Train web-cams on pets and other animals to offer children (or adults adopting endangered animals) the chance to monitor the objects of their affection on a web page or on their mobile phones. Any number of people could share access to any one animal, thereby creating a community or club that could share experiences and support each other if the animal fell ill or died, as is sadly inevitable at some point.

David Owen
22 April 2001

191

Publish a book of the seven or so stories referred to by critics and academics when claiming that there are 'only so many stories ever told'. These narratives – boy meets girl, pride comes before a fall, etc – would be described in generic terms. The book could be marketed as the 'only book you ever need to read' and could list all the other books, films and operas with plotlines derived from each principle narrative.

Chas Bayfield
23 April 2001

192

Produce all-in-one kits for people entering traumatic stages of life. Packs may include the First Period Kit comprising a hot water bottle, ibuprofen, tissues and chocolate; the Puberty Kit including spot cream, cleanser, tissues and books on sex and relationships; the Bereavement Kit complete with black armband, photo-frames and tissues. The packs, which could be sponsored by Kleenex (as all the crucial stages seem to require their products), would make the perfect gifts for family or friends wanting help, while also sparing them the embarrassment of talking about the subject.

Jonathan Lake
24 April 2001

Assemble a mobile phone orchestra. In contrast to typical concert performances, the audience would be asked to ensure that all mobile phones be switched on during the performance. The audience would enter their phone numbers on arrival and musical elements would be sent to each phone as ringtones. The performer on stage would then play a modified keyboard that would place calls to the audience to create an electronic symphony.

Tristan Spill
26 April 2001

Develop a software programme that, in conjunction with a domestic scanner, could recognise leaf shapes from thousands of common plants. The software would be packaged with an encyclopaedia of plants on the web allowing users to identify the plant and view instructions for its care. The software could be used by new homeowners to identify plants in their gardens but also in a more general educational fashion by children returning from country walks. A handheld scanner could be developed to scan leaves without their removal.

Davey Moore
27 April 2001

195

Develop a baton for conductors that could record its own movement during a performance. A software programme could then render the movements in colours or patterns to create a visual interpretation of a piece of music. The resulting visuals could either be screened during a performance or shown as standalone artworks.

Dan Friedman
28 April 2001

196

Mount windmills to the exterior of train carriages to convert the wind power to electricity and power the laptops or walkmans of the passengers.

Steve James
29 April 2001

Editor's note:
This always was daft but now Virgin trains' introduction of plug sockets on carriages has rendered it even more ridiculous.

197

Editor's note:
Wayne Hemingway actually made up some Hair Hats when featuring Idea A Day on The Big Breakfast. We are still waiting for them to appear in the small ads in the back of The Mail On Sunday.

Design a range of hats fashioned from human hair that do not attempt to look in anyway like a full head of hair, but would rather be styled as trilbies, berets or the like. Hair Hats would appeal to people who are honest about their baldness but still keen to enjoy the sensation of having hair on their heads.

Trevor Webb
30 April 2001

198

Design exercise machines for gyms that monitor an individual's heartbeat and play music in time with that beat through headphones. The beats per minute would either track the exerciser's heartbeat as they change pace or could be set at a certain rate, which the individual would attempt to match.

Chas Bayfield
2 May 2001

199

Design tyre treads that incorporate a company logo (the Nike swoosh for example) or even the driver's own signature. The concept could appeal to mountain bike or BMX riders as a kind of ground level graffiti or tagging.

Rupert Kaye
3 May 2001

200

Design personal stereo headphones that incorporate hidden microphones to continually record the surrounding sound. The headphones would allow the wearer to instantly playback speech that was directed toward them but they were unable to hear because they were listening to music. The headphones would also allow the wearer to eavesdrop on conversations that were perhaps held in the confidence that the wearer could not possibly overhear them.

David Owen
4 May 2001

Design teddy bears that could record a toddler's speech. The Diary Bear would ask a child a series of questions about their day; how they feel or their favourite things. Responses would be recorded as digital audio files and date stamped to provide a private record of a child's development.

Sam Torme
5 May 2001

Launch a breakfast cereal for children called 'Smithereens'. The packaging would show an image of a physical object such as a car or a boat exploding toward the customer. The packs would contain bite-sized wreckage, complete with recognisable elements such as seats or a steering wheel, for example.

Dan Friedman
6 May 2001

203

Establish a professional photography or surveillance service to record marriage proposals. The photographers would work covertly to record the proposal and the result, without spoiling the moment. Photographers would only charge if the proposal was successful but should be guaranteed the wedding commission in return.

Rupert Kaye
8 May 2001

204

Launch a range of wallpaper called Wallpeeler. The paper would consist of a number of layered papers featuring contrasting designs. When a homeowner tired of a pattern they would simply peel back the top layer to reveal the fresh print underneath.

Jim Richards
9 May 2001

Create interactive billboards that display advertisements appropriate to the people in the immediate vicinity. The companies controlling the billboards would be fed GPS location information from mobile phone operators as to the whereabouts of their customers. Each person's mobile phone account would be translated as a consumer profile based on their postcode, billing tariff and phone usage. Adverts could then be served to individuals or to appeal to the majority of the potential audience at any one time.

Steve James
10 May 2001

Develop electronic-speech software for dogs, cats or other animals. A device strapped to the dog would monitor the animal's heartbeat, tail wagging and other recognisable body language. The physical signals would trigger appropriate phrases to be called up from a pre-loaded library of sound files. When a dog owner returned from a day at work, for example, their pet would excitedly greet them, saying, 'Boy, am I glad to see you!'

David Owen
11 May 2001

Organise the population of the world into four groups or houses, which would each be represented by a colour. From an agreed start date, each day and therefore each birth date would be assigned a colour in consecutive order and then repeated. The system would aim to create a sense of belonging and community between members of each house that would transcend national borders, race, class and religion.

Chas Bayfield
14 May 2001

Design pushchairs that gently exercise a child's legs. The movement of the wheels would activate pedals or footplates, which would raise one leg and then the other at a set pace. The mechanism would aid a young child to develop the muscles required for walking and discourage laziness in older children.

Mary Slim
15 May 2001

Editor's note:
Ironically, for the growing child, as soon as they were able to peddle themselves they would be forced to get out and walk.

209

Offer a library of ambient sound recordings for mobile phone users to select as a sound bed for their calls. Callers could choose to play the sounds of an airport, a taxi cab or a typical office environment in order to support an excuse for lateness or to throw a pursuer off their trail, perhaps.

Jim Richards
16 May 2001

210

Design a theme-park style attraction on which visitors can ride in their own cars. The ride would be less physically exhilarating than a roller coaster but could be enhanced by a 360-degree film projection and a soundtrack played directly from a dedicated radio station into the cars. Following the ride, visitors would be offered pictures of themselves driving their own cars through incredible landscapes.

Dan Friedman
17 May 2001

Design a computer game for PCs in which monsters appear from holes positioned in line with the standard layout of a QWERTY keyboard. Whatever a player typed in their attempt to strike the monsters would appear on screen. Smart players could therefore read as they played and predict where monsters would next appear by guessing the endings to words and sentences.

David Owen
19 May 2001

Design spectacle frames that change colour on demand. Using fibre optics or propelled ink, the glasses could change from jet-black, to clear and to red, for example, offering wearers multiple pairs for a single purchase.

Steve James
20 May 2001

Introduce double beds to hospitals. The terminally ill would be able to spend their final days close to their partners, and poorly infants would be comforted by the familiar presence of their parents.

Justin Hawkins
21 May 2001

Broadcast commentaries on sports events provided by the sportsmen and women actually competing in games and matches. A golfer could comment on his opponent's drive while waiting to take his own shot, for example. These unique insights into the game could be provided on dedicated television or radio stations with competitors paid for everything they say.

Mary Slim
22 May 2001

Produce special package designs for products that would reflect and support common secondary usages of the packaging by children. Yoghurt pots could be graphically styled as high-tech walkie-talkies and sold in packs of two complete with string. The standard brand and content information would be integrated into the designs. A washing up liquid bottle might be designed to look like a space rocket with the brand name taking the place of NASA on the exterior.

Dan Friedman
23 May 2001

Introduce customer league tables for shopping. Customers keen on particular brands can choose to be represented by their full name, a nickname or an anonymous code in the tables. Points would be awarded based directly on the value of purchases made. Global customer bases could be broken down demographically such that an individual could claim, or aspire, to be Nike's best under-15 customer in their hometown.

Editor's note:
This rather direct idea may well have been tried before. It was certainly not, as far as we can recall from history lessons, a feature of any Communist manifestos or five-year plans.

David Owen
24 May 2001

217

Launch a range of household paints under the name of PopPaints. Each colour or shade would be inspired, or personally mixed, by current teenage favourites. Young fans could then put up posters of their idols on their specially painted bedroom walls.

Justin Cooke
25 May 2001

218

Create a digital television station for the blind, on which an audio commentary would be broadcast over the soundtrack of each programme. The commentary would describe the action, the expressions on peoples' faces and other visual clues that unsighted and visually impaired people would miss. The commentary would be discreet so as not to interfere with the natural dialogue. Cinemas could make use of this feature by installing an audio channel, which would be picked up by headphones.

Chas Bayfield
26 May 2001

Launch an interactive television game show called 'Make Me Laugh' in which the viewers would be invited to submit jokes in an attempt to make the presenters laugh. Should the collective audience succeed in cracking up one presenter, another more stony-faced presenter would be introduced. More extreme versions of the format such as 'Make Me Blush' or 'Make Me Cry' could also be developed.

Mary Slim
27 May 2001

Editor's note:
'Make Me Laugh' would be particularly interesting in that it would test a theory that the combined efforts of thousands of people at home may still not be as funny as one single good television comedian.

Release a range of disposable cameras on which one picture would already have been taken. For example, a camera styled and branded as merchandising for a particular pop act could include an exclusive picture of the star on each roll. Advertisers could also employ the cameras in competitions. Cameras could include a picture showing one part of a map or one digit from a telephone number that, when completed, would lead customers to a prize.

Dan Friedman
28 May 2001

Develop a system that could customise and print town and city maps according to an individual's requirements. Tourist attractions, cashpoint machines, pubs or hotels would dynamically appear on the personal maps and other features of less interest could be deselected on the user's request.

Justin Cooke
30 May 2001

Editor's note:
Unfortunately, this concept seems to have been adopted most enthusiastically be telesales companies and should probably be made illegal if it is not already.

Introduce a domestic or mobile telephone service that would allow enable callers to dial a group of friends at the same time. The caller would be connected to the first person to pick up the phone. The service could be used to avoid making a series of calls to answer machines in search of someone to talk with. It could also be used as a mechanism for personal competitions. Someone with a cinema ticket to spare, for example, could offer it to the first friend to answer. Friends who heard the phone ring but picked up too late would hear a recorded message telling them who was calling and where they were placed in the race to respond.

David Owen
31 May 2001

Design a pair of 'Magnifying Gloves'. The fabric of the gloves would consist of hundreds of sensors on the exterior and probes or electrons on the inside. When an object is held or touched by a gloved hand, a certain number of sensors will be directly engaged, while neighbouring sensors will be automatically activated, giving the wearer the sensation of holding or touching a larger object. The gloves would have an obvious role to play in sexual practices, whether for couples or gentlemen acting on their own.

Mary Slim
2 June 2001

Create Infopromos: music videos that could be made in Flash for viewing via the web. As rock songs or pieces of classical music were played, the screen would present text-based information such as the inspiration for the song, a biography of the composer or an explanation of the lyrics. Diagrams, illustrations and photographs could also be used to demonstrate key changes, for example, or to show the exact models of guitars being played.

Dan Friedman
3 June 2001

Editor's note:
*Sam Torme's
inspiration for this
admittedly pointless
idea was drawn from
an episode of
Bagpuss in which
Charlie Mouse and his
friends operate a mill
that makes chocolate
biscuits simply taking
the same biscuit out
of one end and
putting it back in the
other.*

Launch a spoof Internet company offering free paper. Customers who click to receive the free paper would actually be activating their printer to print out a sheet of their own existing supply with the message 'Thank you for shopping at InstantPaper.com' at the bottom.

Sam Torme
4 June 2001

Open a chain of bars or nightclubs offering the public the chance to perform stripteases. These karaoke strip clubs would require exemption from local public indecency laws and would attract a large expectant crowd and the occasional exhibitionist.

David Owen
5 June 2001

227

Produce a television chat show in which politicians would be interviewed whilst wired up to lie detectors. If a guest lied twice they would be ejected and the airtime handed to a member of an opposing party.

Becky Clarke
7 June 2001

228

Introduce commercials to the theatre. The time before the curtain goes up and during the intermission would present great opportunities for advertisers. Theatre Ads would be performed live on stage either by the actors or the understudies from the main show.

Trevor Webb
8 June 2001

229

Editor's note:
Shortly after publishing this idea, we did see drawings somewhere for a garden fence panel that could be rotated into a horizontal position to offer a table tennis surface for neighbour versus neighbour match play.

Design retractable garden fencing. Such fencing would be ideal for friendly neighbours who wish to roll back the divide and share a larger garden space. If one neighbour went on holiday, the other could have both gardens to themselves. Rolling back a whole street of fences would create a park for all residents.

Chas Bayfield
11 June 2001

230

Introduce cameras with a small handheld remote button allowing the subject of a photograph to take the picture. The photographer behind the camera would compose the picture, but the subject would take the final decision as to exactly when they felt personally composed and ready to be captured.

Mike Sawdon
13 June 2001

231

Design a utility belt with in-built drinks holsters. The belt would be marketed towards the labour industries, where workers regularly use both hands in quite thirsty work. The belt could also be worn socially and would be particularly useful in crowded bars. Drinkers would be free to roam the bar, smoke cigarettes or play fruit machines without ever putting down their drink. A gravity-based tilt mechanism could be employed to avoid spillage when leaning over a pool table.

Lee Tatham
14 June 2001

232

Develop an amplification system for bicycles such that they can be made to sound like cars or motorbikes. The engine sounds would serve to make cycling safer as drivers and pedestrians would hear them coming. Children, of course, would be less concerned with the safety benefits than with experiencing a simulated motorbike ride.

James Hamilton
15 June 2001

Editor's note:
There are numerous existing means for kids to customise bikes and create engine sounds. No method ever worked better that simply tucking the front rubber mudguard on a 1980's Raleigh Grifter back in on itself (at least until it completely disintegrated).

233

Design polo-neck jumpers with very long necks that can be rolled up over the head. Holes for the eyes and mouth would be cut from the neck. The new balaclava jumper would make for a stylish and efficient garment for the more sartorial villain or SAS operative.

Sam Torme
17 June 2001

234

Write a software application called 'Internet Explorers' that would allow users to explore the web and place flags on sites to claim their discovery. Other users who download the application would be able to see the flags when visiting the same sites. Journeys undertaken by the Internet Explorers could be recorded on a central site along with their commentaries and act as travelogues.

David Owen
18 June 2001

234

Develop a golf game to be played across the web. Represented by an animated golfer, users would strike the ball from the tee-off page and follow its trajectory across a landscape of consecutive pages. The means of navigation around the web could either be purely random, via Google or Yahoo, or predetermined by sponsorship deals with companies looking to promote their sites by placing holes on their homepages.

Dan Friedman
20 June 2001

235

Develop voice-activated software that automatically enters spoken words into search engines and presents the best URL from the search results on screen. The software could be employed in a brainstorming meeting to continually interpret the conversation and illustrate ideas under discussion on a screen. It could also be used to novelty effect in a bar or restaurant, offering a visual interpretation of conversations held privately in booths for other drinkers and diners to watch.

Mary Slim
21 June 2001

Editor's note:
This idea could work very well. Tests in which spoken words and dialogue were swiftly typed into Google's 'Get Lucky' feature genuinely yielded interesting and enlightening results.

Design a pedal toilet where, by default, the toilet seat is down. When a male intended to use the toilet from a standing position, they would simply step on a pedal (much like the ones found on a pedal bin) which would lift the seat and smoothly return it to the closed position when the foot was removed.

Zak Mcflimby
22 June 2001

Editor's note:
The Internet as a fantasy parallel universe? All those perennially single men that used to play Dungeons & Dragons in the '80s could have told us that ages ago.

Develop software that creates unique cartoon monsters from the properties of web pages. Code would be written to interpret elements of a page's design; the primary colours employed, fonts, images and so on, into physical attributes of a character or monster. Each monster would not only look different but would also be imbued with particular strengths or weaknesses. Users could then have their monsters battle each other (Amazon monster v. MSN monster). Site owners would be able to reverse-engineer the code through trial and error in order to design web pages that generate powerful monsters.

Chris O'Brien
23 June 2001

Develop software for DVD players that would enable the home viewer to turn off the set or change channel by shooting at the television screen with an electronic gun. The firearms could be used to vent frustration and boredom when viewing a bad or disappointing film. If the hits and misses were recorded and uploaded to a server they could also be the basis for multiplayer competitions. Special editions of films such as Star Wars they could be released for the home audience to fire at the baddies.

David Owen
25 June 2001

Offer a mobile ringtone service with which customers can purchase a ringtone and send it to a friend under a title of their own choosing. They may simply write 'Thinking of you' when sending the melodies of 'Just Can't Get Enough', 'Glad to be Gay' or other songs that ironically comment on their friend's character or fortunes.

Dan Friedman
26 June 2001

Introduce a new packaging for sweets, crisps, and other snacks offered in cinemas that would make no discernable sound when handled. Discreet sweets would be wrapped in a softer plastic, while crisp bags would employ an air valve release to deter laptop explosions.

Becky Clarke
27 June 2001

Editor's note:
An idea not entirely dissimilar from the stretch, reach and grab test posed by the top-shelf positioning of other men's magazines.

Develop a promotion for a men's fitness or lifestyle magazine wherein each magazine would be shrink-wrapped with a particularly strong plastic. The magazine cover would urge readers to take the challenge of tearing the wrapper open with their bare hands and report inside on the results of the strength test.

Sam Torme
28 June 2001

Design a T-shirt with a simple textual design, which would read 'www.buytheshirt.com'. The URL would deliver a single page website on which the shirt would be available for purchase.

Mary Slim
29 June 2001

Launch a broadband Internet news bulletin that would feature a well-known television newsreader but could also be personalised by the viewer. Visitors to the bulletin's website would be invited to type their own personal news, such as birth or marriage announcements into a text-to-speech engine to create their own unique clip, which they could send to friends. The actual news headlines of the day would open the bulletin, before the newsreader added, 'And finally...'

Sam Torme
4 July 2001

245

Editor's note:
Presumably the service would be self-perpetuating as anyone objecting to a message could only erase it by publishing something of their own.

Launch a public access ad-banner server on the web. A digital white board would be hosted on a central site allowing anyone to type anything they wanted into the banner space. Each entry would wipe off the last but would also be posted across the Internet on all participating sites and the desktops/screensavers of individual subscribers. The service would be free of censorship, allowing users to advertise any services or express political or social messages as they saw fit.

Mary Slim
5 July 2001

Editor's note:
This game inspired another idea for a Country Of The Year Awards. One of the last to be included in this book.

Introduce International Trumps, a Top Trump game based on the strengths and weaknesses of countries around the world. Categories could include supermodels per thousand of the population, number of great inventions, sporting achievements, great composers, wars initiated and wars won.

Alex Wilson-Smith
7 July 2001

Introduce a website with a scrolling news feed describing the twists and turns of daytime television soap operas. Fans of the programmes with office jobs would be able to stay in touch quite discreetly with plotlines as they unravelled. A chat facility would also be offered such that the office-based audience could ask specific questions relating to what the characters were wearing, or the expressions on actors' faces, to truly hardcore fans who might be watching the show and online at the same time.

David Owen
8 July 2001

Develop an SMS text game that would be synchronised to television programmes as they are first broadcast. Players of the game would watch programmes in an attempt to spot certain clues; when a character said a particular word or when stars made surprise cameo appearances. Answers would be sent by text and a cumulative score could be attributed to each viewer. At the end of a series the biggest and best fans of any programme would be announced and rewarded.

Sam Torme
9 July 2001

249

Editor's note:
*Not the most subtle
or even morally
acceptable of ideas
but Mary Slim tells it
straight. This is
probably a more
workable version of
David Owen's
shopping league
tables from 24 May
2001.*

Encourage even greater use of mobile phones by children and teenagers by recording the number of calls received by individual users and drawing up customer league tables. Positional information could be sent back to users via SMS. People with the highest number of calls received would, of course, be deemed the most popular, which may well provide incentive enough for some people to elevate their positions by repeatedly calling themselves.

Mary Slim
10 July 2001

250

Design Santa's Beard baby bibs. These plastic or cloth bibs would attach to the child's ears and cover the chin and upper lip, thereby saving parental face wiping following a meal. The bibs would be overprinted with an illustrated or photographic image of a curly white beard.

Dan Friedman
14 July 2001

251

Introduce a celebrity-spotting service for users of mobile camera phones. Pictures taken of celebrities would be automatically time and date stamped and attributed coordinates by GPS. The amateur paparazzi could send the pictures to a central server where they would be immediately sent to all subscribers of the service within twenty miles of the sighting.

David Owen
15 July 2001

252

Launch the concept of 'Air Cuts' – a hair cut in every way other than that the customer's hair is untouched. The stylist or barber would cut either with their fingers or with scissors held an inch clear of the customer's head. The service may well appeal to bald or lonely people who wish to spend a little time in good company, discussing what they did on the weekend and where they are going on holiday.

Sam Torme
16 July 2001

Editor's note:
Toby Gunton preferred the idea of 'Silent Cuts' for customers who do need a trim but really don't want to talk at all.

253

Launch a media agency to sell advertising space on the reverse of company letterheads and notepaper. A company of electricians, for example, might sell ads to plumbers or builder's merchants on the reverse of their printed estimates.

Chas Bayfield
17 July 2001

254

Editor's note:
We like the idea that phone users around the world, from pre-teens to business executives, could be working together to keep a ball in the air for a day or a week across various time zones.

Create a soccer 'keep-ups' game for mobile phones. The screen would display the image of a star footballer. The keys on the keypad would correspond to parts of the player's body; 1 for the right shoulder, 9 for left foot etc. The object of the game would be to keep the ball in the air for as long as possible. On a 3G network, gamers would be able to see their scores in a national league table and even pass the ball from one phone screen to another.

Mary Slim
18 July 2001

Introduce a fishing game for mobile phones in which an incoming call represents a bite on the line. The source of the call (local, same mobile network, international) would determine the type of fish and the duration of the call would determine the size and weight of the catch. SMS text messages would follow each call to report the catch and players would be able to compete against each other.

Dan Friedman
20 July 2001

Editor's note:
This idea was inspired by a much cuter idea which unfortunately we didn't think of first. A Scandinavian mobile operator introduced an SMS fishing game in which players simply registered, did nothing for a few hours and then, if they were lucky, their phone would bleep with a text informing them of their catch.

Launch a subscription SMS game in which instructions for distinctive physical actions are sent simultaneously to many players by text. A section of the subscriber base may be requested to put their hand up and show three fingers. Another set may be asked to perform windmills with their right arm. Other gamers would have to spot or make a guess as to the actions within five minutes of the instruction being sent.

Charles Cohen
22 July 2001

257

Design mugs for coffee or tea that can be personalised by the owner. The mugs would be sold with a permanent pen, which would be used to state the owner's name and complete tick boxes to indicate how they prefer their drinks to be made. The mugs would make ideal gifts for people to personalise and then give to their colleagues at work with a heavy hint.

David Apps
24 July 2001

258

Erect statues of people who have died in road accidents at the scenes of the incidents. Families of the deceased could choose between figurative representations or symbolic structures. The statues would constitute a very strong reminder to motorists and pedestrians to take care and drive responsibly.

Chas Bayfield
25 July 2001

259

Design business cards as scratch cards. The individual's job title, private line or mobile number could be hidden behind a silver panel. Cards could feature a game in which the scratch-off panel reveals different levels of interaction or response – lunch at The Ivy or a promise to return phone calls within an hour, perhaps.

Angela Hill
26 July 2001

260

Create software that reads or listens to a phone user's text messages or conversation (with the permission of the caller, of course) and responds in a sympathetic fashion. A 3G phone could allow all calls to be monitored by software on a web server. If the software recognises the phrase 'I love you' spoken by a caller, the phone itself could turn red, start vibrating and play Stevie Wonder's 'I just called to say...' as a ringtone or MP3.

Dan Friedman
27 July 2001

261

Design a universal-plug tie. This geek fashion accessory could be worn in corporate IT environments and would be the Swiss army knife of cabling. Whenever there was a need for a cable the wearer would simply lean in with their tie and connect the two points.

Tristan Spill
28 July 2001

262

Design a small, floating balloon to enable toddlers to play and practise tennis strokes. The balloon would be as close to the size of a standard tennis ball as possible and filled with a mixture of helium and oxygen such that it would float, without floating away.

Mary Slim
29 July 2001

263

Establish a financially independent order of nuns. The nuns would find employment in positions where their appearance and beliefs would present them with an advantage over other applicants. Nuns employed as security guards or nightclub bouncers, for example, would no doubt have a positive effect on the criminal or violent tendencies of the general public.

Chas Bayfield
30 July 2001

264

Produce a daily newspaper for the café society. Each morning, two A4 pages of news headlines and top stories would be published on the Internet for download as PDF files. Cafe owners would print the pages back-to-back and laminate them before distributing to tables. A dedicated media agency would manage the placement of local advertising, which would be published on the pages dependent on the location of the host café.

Dean Scott
31 July 2001

285

Launch a new premium beer brand that would be more expensive than competing beers but would include, in the price of each pint, a contribution to a pension plan for the customer. The brand could offer either a dedicated loyalty or credit card or make a deal with existing cards such that the contributions would not be the responsibility of the pub or bar.

Richard Jackson
1 August 2001

286

Launch a premium-rate phone-line for football supporters to call while matches are being played. Fans would call into a switchboard, identify the game they were interested in and be put through to another fan, who would actually be at the game. The supporter in the ground could answer any questions or provide a personal commentary. The amateur commentators would receive credits on their account in return for taking calls.

David Owen
2 August 2001

Determine one memorable telephone number for use in all advertising campaigns offering further information regarding brands or products. Rather than having to remember different freephone numbers, customers would simply call the advertising enquiries number and quote the company name to be put through to the correct line. The advertiser would have to cover the cost of the calls such that the customer would not be charged.

Jim Bolton
4 August 2001

Editor's note:
It is worth noting that this idea was written and published well before the deregulation of directory enquiries service. That being well before the advertising of phone numbers itself became a national media obsession.

Introduce a non-toxic fluorescent ingredient into dog food. At night, dog excrement would be illuminated, warning the unsuspecting pedestrian and turning the most drab street into a veritable promenade of colour.

Jeff Lyons
5 August 2001

Design electronic tags for clothing with memory chips that hold data describing the colour, mix of materials and year of design of the garment. Owners of such clothing could assemble outfits and request the chips to check with each other to determine if the various garments clash or coordinate. As an example, socks would trigger an alarm when introduced to sandals.

Dan Friedman
6 August 2001

Editor's note:
It is worth explaining that Idea A Day and The Big Idea Book operate a policy under which ideas that the editorial team may not wish to encourage and may even find offensive are published if it is felt they could actually be popular with others or in some way inspire other more positive ideas.

Devise a location-based SMS text game using GPS in which registered players would be given an arsenal of virtual bombs and explosives that could be detonated in public by sending a text message to a shortcode. The messages would be received by a server, which would calculate the number of players within the blast area of the explosion at that specific time. This total would be credited to the mobile terrorist, while each player hit would lose a point or a life.

Sam Torme
7 August 2001

Create a mobile phone massage-game. The head and neck of a male or female model would be displayed on the mobile screen, while numbers and function buttons on the phone would correspond directly to areas of the subject's body. Pressing buttons in a particular sequence or with a certain frequency would elicit either a positive or negative response from the subject. Masseurs could play while calling a premium rate number such that they could actually hear the moans, groans or yelps of pain they are triggering.

David Owen
9 August 2001

Editor's note:
The note for idea 270 applies equally to this idea.

Manufacture a miniature plastic secretary or intern that would record office gossip and play it back by means of an internal digital-recording device. The secretary would be centrally placed or passed around an office. Workers would whisper their gossip into the secretary's ear, after which it would tell them everyone else's in return.

Alex Wilson-Smith
11 August 2001

273

Open a restaurant with a biblical theme called 'The Garden of Eatin'. The menu would include Adam's barbecue ribs or giblets with fig leaves, while the waitresses would use all their powers of persuasion in recommending the apple pie.

Rachel Mize
12 August 2001

274

Editor's note:
This almost sci-fi concept was inspired by the 'send a postcard' features that are quite popular on many children's websites. We still haven't worked out whether it is simply the child's youth and naivety that leads them to believe that a website is an actual desination or whether the same generation will grow up with this understanding.

Create a software system that locates friends or colleagues by cyber-location rather than geographical location. A user would send a query regarding the whereabouts of a friend by email, text or instant message. If the friend chose to disclose their whereabouts, they would simply click 'yes' and the system would return their location by URL (i.e. browsing for jazz CDs at Amazon.com). On receipt of a response, the enquirer could click to join their friend and continue their conversation with a shared reference point.

Dan Friedman
13 August 2001

Launch a file-sharing or download-based enterprise that would offer its content for free but would charge users for memory cards or additional hard drives. The additional memory would be proprietary and encrypted such that the downloaded files could only be stored and accessed from the company's hardware.

Martin Searle
14 August 2001

Launch a website to trace the origins of popular jokes and urban myths. Jokes would be published on the site for users to add the date at which they think they first heard them and a note disclosing the source from which they were heard. A reverse email-chain system could also be developed to track back a popular office-email gag. The site could feature an Amazon styled 'Are you the author?' option to save time and effort.

Chas Bayfield
15 August 2001

Editor's note:
Someone, somewhere and at sometime must have written or said, 'A horse walks into a bar and the barman says, "Why the long face?"'. That person deserves as much credit and praise as the most successful of comedians and comic writers.

Launch a brand of glow-in-the-dark cigarettes. Called 'Illuminettes', the cigarettes would be sold at clubs and concerts as a novelty night-time accessory and would look most striking when waved in the air by dancers.

Justin Cooke
17 August 2001

Design a range of headphones shaped like real ears, which could be worn over the user's own. Popular designs might include ears shaped like those permanently sported by Spock, Prince Charles or Dumbo the Elephant.

Alex Wilson-Smith
18 August 2001

279

Introduce cash rewards for citizens who stay on the right side of the law. If the rewards were great enough they could become self-financing, as the substantial costs to the state incurred by criminal acts, legal cases and imprisonment would be reduced.

Rupert Kaye
19 August 2001

Editor's note:
Pity the government minister that introduces this bill only to get caught speeding on the way back to his/her constituency.

280

Launch a website that would publish personal reports of road accidents and driving incidents. Comments and accusations could be sent via text message from the roads or, after due consideration, by email. Anonymity would be offered on the site but not if the postings were required as evidence in court or for insurance settlements. For those written about, the site would act as a fully interactive version of the 'How's my driving?' phone numbers displayed on commercial vehicles.

Al Tepper
22 August 2001

Editor's note:
Obviously in the light of recent legislation, we should emphasise that drivers should not text whilst driving lest they incur the wrath of the law, cause an accident and end up being reported to this web site themselves.

Devise a national 'unlucky lottery'. Events and occurrences normally considered to be unfortunate would be the point of entry to the lottery and would therefore become more of an opportunity than a mishap. A CCTV camera could be set up to record one in every ten people who walk under a ladder, for example, or the first person each day to arrive at an airport check-in without their passport. Tickets would be on sale every week and cash prizes would only be paid out to unlucky individuals holding a valid ticket at the time of their accident or incident.

Sam Torme
23 August 2001

Launch a table-sitting service for individuals and groups who wish to secure tables or positions at the bar in busy pubs, bars and cafes. Sitters would charge by the hour to occupy a table with nominal expenses to cover half-hourly mineral waters.

Chas Bayfield
24 August 2001

283

Launch a telephone service on which children's stories are narrated. The 'Phone Book' would offer a bookmark feature for children to listen to long stories over a succession of calls.

Rupert Kaye
25 August 2001

284

Design a novelty television remote-control in the form of a gun. If retro-styled as a revolver, viewers could spin the barrel through the EPG and pull the trigger to select channels. By changing channels, viewers would feel like they were blowing away the disappointing programme they were watching.

Chas Bayfield
27 August 2001

285

Offer a 'change of life' service in the style of a voluntary witness relocation program. For a substantial fee, customers would be provided with a new identity, passport, home, career and the opportunity to reinvent themselves.

Rupert Kaye
30 August 2001

286

Editor's note:
If this idea doesn't find its way to becoming the next viral email craze we give up.

Develop novelty autocue software for office computer screens. Rather than the news headlines or party political broadcasts, the office version would scroll scripts for situations such as asking out co-workers, negotiating a pay rise or even firing someone.

Sam Torme
3 September 2001

287

Produce a novelty mobile for children featuring a number of brightly coloured mobile phones that slowly revolve above a cot while playing a selection of popular ringtones.

David Owen
5 September 2001

288

Invent an alarm clock that scans local radio traffic broadcasts and weather forecasts and adjusts the alarm time accordingly. If traffic was really bad, the alarm might sound an hour early. If it was raining heavily on a weekend, it probably wouldn't ring at all.

Dan Jarrold
7 September 2001

Editor's note:
This Idea A Day favourite inspired another related concept, wherein alarm clocks could be set remotely by friends and colleagues who have been entrusted with passwords.

Launch a website offering immediate translations of foreign language news stories and articles. The service would come into its own the day after, for example, England had beaten Germany at football. A match report from Die Zeitung would suddenly become the subject of much gloating interest in the UK.

Dan Friedman
10 September 2001

Establish the points of shared belief or general agreement between the world's major religions. These points of common ground could be published as an entry point to religion for children or those whose faith has lapsed.

Chas Bayfield
12 September 2001

Introduce a telephone service for busy, forgetful or self-obsessed individuals to maintain the illusion that they are concerned about their friends. Once a month, the user would record a generic voice message along the lines of 'Hi! Just wondering how you are?' They would then enter the phone numbers of friends and acquaintances. The service would dial the numbers until an answer machine was reached and would then leave the message. Should a friend actually answer the phone, the system would play back one of a large selection of recordings of vaguely foreign people explaining that they have the wrong number.

Sam Torme
16 September 2001

Launch a new cable or digital television channel called 'The Random Channel'. The channel would broadcast much the same fare as its competitors but would never publish schedules or listings. The channel could run an ad campaign with the strap line: 'You don't know what you're missing'.

David Owen
17 September 2001

Editor's note:
A similar result can be created simply by flipping through channels with no regard to television listings. Allegedly, this is how the male half of the population prefers to watch television anyway.

Design clear plastic shoes to be sold together with pairs of special socks. The socks would sport typical patterns down to the ankle while the part covered by the shoe would be designed to appear like brown suede, black leather or any shoe material desired. In this fashion, the same pair of shoes could be worn with suits or trousers of varying colour and style.

Charles Addison
18 September 2001

Devise a fruit machine game to be played on multiple mobile phones. Players would line up their phones and request to play. Picture messages bearing cherries or bars and the like would be sent to the phones. Each game would be charged to the individual's phone bill but the cash prizes for lines could be shared between all players in a session. The number of players would be unlimited and the prize money would escalate accordingly. The game could also be played remotely with the other player's results shown as thumbnail images, or as a single player game, with three reels on the same screen.

David Owen
24 September 2001

295

Open a restaurant for diners on Slimfast and other recognised diets. The menu would consist purely of Slimfast milkshakes and other meals recommended by diet plans. The restaurant would provide a pleasant sociable ambiance for people who would otherwise be sitting at home or behind a desk. Staff would serve customers in the usual generous fashion but could also enforce diners' individual quotas if they were asked to do so in advance.

Chas Bayfield
25 September 2001

Editor's note:
Charles Cohen was quick to demonstrate how this concept had dated: 'This idea was clearly pre-Atkins. The problem now is that putting a group of Atkins dieters in the same confined space is almost certain to result in bloodshed as the crazed fools take chunks out of each other, driven mad by their carbohydrate deprivation.'

296

Design a breast-enlarging knitwear range for women. The jumpers and cardigans would be closely knit with double or triple stitching subtly introduced to the bust.

Charles Addison
27 September 2001

Design an ultra-light aluminium pilot to ride ahead of trains. A chip in the front end of the train would control the speed of the pilot such that the distance between train and pilot carrier would be equal to the distance the train needs to break. If anything should happen to the pilot or the wireless signal between the pilot and train, the train would automatically break and stop just before colliding with the cause of the problem. Head-on collisions would be averted if both trains were fitted with the device.

Remi Beukers
28 September 2001

Develop a method of printing T-shirts such that the designs fade or wash away over a specific period of time. These transient designs would be particularly appropriate for celebrating the short careers of teeny pop groups, or the success of a national football team in the World Cup. The shirts themselves could be reprinted many times over before they actually wear out.

David Owen
29 September 2001

299

Devise an arcade game in which a player takes on the role of an invisible man, attempting to navigate his way on foot across a major city such as Los Angeles or New York without being hit by cars or other pedestrians who would be unaware of their position or movement.

Chas Bayfield
1 October 2001

300

Market fingerprint-dusting kits and macro lens cameras to the public with a view to creating a trade in celebrity fingerprints. The prints of notable individuals could be published on the Internet for verification by amateur dusters all over the world. Celebrities might even welcome the practice, as the participation required of them (opening a door or drinking from a glass) would be significantly less taxing than signing their names.

Dan Friedman
2 October 2001

301

Publish a series of new or classic novels in special editions with annotations by critics, celebrities or other relevant individuals printed in the margin.

Sam Torme
3 October 2001

Editor's note:
Television executive David Brook suggested that this was the literary equivalent of 'Beavis and Butthead'. That said, on the evidence of most library copies of Jackie Collins or Harold Robbins and how they seem to fall open just-so, most readers wouldn't need B&B's help to find the naughty bits.

302

Launch of a range of dog or cat foods designed for human ingestion. These tinned quick meals or snack foods could either trade on the recognition and reputation of established pet food brands or simply be styled in a similar fashion. Packaging designs for Pedigree Chum Man would of course feature a healthy male in a shiny coat on the tin.

David Owen
5 October 2001

Devise a multiplayer Shoot 'Em Up game to be played on top of the worldwide web. Software would be downloaded which would allow players to see each other if they visited a website at the same time. Players could hide at remote and obscure amateur web pages or join the fray on popular sites such as MSN or Amazon. The owners of the websites themselves would generally be oblivious to the games being played out on their pages but could join in by inserting graphic elements from the game, such as black holes or landmines, into the design of their pages.

Dan Friedman
9 October 2001

Devise a Truth or Dare game for mobile phones. A handset could be placed between players and then spun. Whomever it pointed to would choose their fate by texting 'truth' or 'dare' to a shortcode number. A question or challenge would then be sent to the phone as a text message.

George Cockerill
12 October 2001

Editor's note:
George Cockerill designed and built the Idea A Day website at Fortune Cookie. Over 14 months we waited for him to come up with an idea. This was his first and it was a gem. As discussed in the introduction, it was in development with a telephone operator the next morning.

305

Editor's note:
*Of course, for an extra
charge it could be
arranged that the
couple are caught by
a police officer...*

Open a hotel without any bedrooms, but which offers instead the private letting of spaces such as offices, vans, lawns and alleyways to amorous couples. Guests could experience the thrill of 'roughing it' without the worry of being caught by their boss, spouse, security or the police.

Davey Moore
13 October 2001

306

Launch a website to store digital passport-style photographs for members of the public. Photo-booths would be introduced to take the pictures and upload them to the site. The site itself would be linked to passport offices, travel companies, universities and other institutions that require photo-ID.

David Owen
15 October 2001

307

Produce alcoholic ice-lollies for night clubbers. The lollies would offer the same alcoholic content as a standard measure but could also be waved around by dancers without spilling and would help them chill out — quite literally. The lolly sticks could be printed with the words 'May I have another?' and could be handed to bar staff when the music was too loud to speak over.

Richard Ryan
17 October 2001

Editor's note:
Jay Pond-Jones applied some rare pragmatism to this idea. He pointed out that alcohol might well freeze at a different temperature to water and that things could get very messy — in every sense.

308

Sell temporary transfers that are exact copies of real tattoos sported by indelible celebrities such as Cher, Robbie Williams or Justin Hawkins.

Davey Moore
18 October 2001

309

Undertake an art project wherein the artist deliberately stands in or walks through the background of other people's snapshot photographs. At a later date, a likeness of the artist could be published in a newspaper with a request for any pictures featuring the interloper to be submitted for inclusion in an exhibition.

Chas Bayfield
20 October 2001

310

Devise an advertising campaign that seeks to capture the public's attention and respect by providing genuinely useful information alongside or within the advertising message. Posters in high street shopping centres might list the nearest department store toilets, and those in underground stations could offer tips on visiting local tourist sites and avoiding crowds.

David Owen
22 October 2001

311

Introduce a subtitled service for viewers of football coverage on digital television that would transcribe the terrace chants of the supporters in the ground. The often offensive and rude subtitles could be made available only to viewers who have offered proof of their age in advance.

Mary Slim
23 October 2001

312

Employ Hotmail or other free email accounts as message boards for nomadic groups of Internet users. A simple email address with an openly published password would be sufficient to create a space for communication. As individuals would have the power to delete messages or change the password, managing the account would require both healthy restraint and consensual policing.

Sam Torme
24 October 2001

Editor's note: This idea has been specially implemented for the publication of this book. The account address is allcomers@hotmail.com and the password is, or at least it once was, 'password'. Good luck with getting in.

Devise a suite of Internet sites to publish the names of everyone in the world. A site set up for the population of the UK, for example, could offer everyone in the country 30 seconds of recognition within 60 years of their birth. Time slots would be booked far enough ahead to give the individual the opportunity to compose a message or personal statement. The site would stream the name checks 24 hours a day and would make for an engaging screensaver.

David Owen
31 October 2001

Introduce designer washing powders or liquids scented with perfumes such as Obsession or Chanel No.5.

Oly Coysh
4 November 2001

315

Open a £1 shop that, rather than retailing items that are discounted to £1, would instead sell high quality examples of goods that are typically priced lower than the £1 denomination. Customers would still be invited to 'have a look around, it's only a pound' but they would find delicious ripe apples, limited edition cans of Coke or perfectly balanced Biro pens on the shelves.

Mary Slim
7 November 2001

316

Produce a range of frozen sandwiches for packed lunches. A month's supply could be bought with the weekly shopping. While defrosting, the sandwich would act as a cool pack within an insulated lunchbox.

Julian Richardson
8 November 2001

Editor's note:
*As Toby Gunton
suggested to us, Dan
Friedman need not
stop here. There is a
whole range of
disgusting foods
waiting to be
launched including
vomit-topped pizzas
and bogey burgers.*

317

Launch an ice cream that is fashioned to look like excrement on a stick. These novel chocolate flavoured ice creams would repulse or delight the public pretty much depending on which side of nineteen years old they fall. The sticks would carry the instruction 'Now please wash your hands'.

Dan Friedman
15 November 2001

318

Launch an open source and possibly copyright-free website on which individuals can post biographical details of fictional characters of their own creation. Authors and scriptwriters could use the site as a resource, while the character sketches could prove entertaining enough to attract an audience of their own.

Sam Torme
19 November 2001

319

Add a new function key (Ctrl+I) for use with all web browsers, Word and other software, which would transform any text into a hyperlink. Users would highlight text and hit the function key. The text would then be submitted to a search engine, and the highest placed search result would be opened up in a new window. The function would be especially useful for quickly verifying names or places referred to in electronic books or online newspaper articles.

Dan Friedman
23 November 2001

320

Devise a television show called 'When Kids Get Caught' in which a camera crew would follow leads provided by snitch school friends to capture footage of young people breaking the law and being apprehended. Suitably embarrassing but entertaining crimes may include petty shoplifting, truancy and underage drinking.

David Owen
24 November 2001

Editor's note:
It was hoped that this idea might actually help to deter juvenile lawbreaking. On reflection, it would probably have quite the opposite effect as getting on the television is probably even more of an attraction for kids than nicking dirty mags and smoking the odd cigarette.

321

Launch a premium-rate telephone service called Talk To A Stranger. Calls to the line would be connected to a randomly selected domestic telephone number. A recorded message would explain to whomever picked up the phone that the caller was paying, say, 50p a minute and that a share of the revenue would be credited to their phone bill should they accept the call.

Sam Torme
25 November 2001

322

Subsidise the economy by introducing advertising messages to bank notes and coins. Advertisers could take the opportunity to explain how the particular denomination could be spent on their products. Should the concept prove too blatantly commercial for public acceptance, the currency could be employed to communicate charitable statements and requests. A description of what £10 could buy in a struggling third-world economy would make quite an impression if printed on a bank note.

Mary Slim
27 November 2001

323

Introduce a personal shopping service in which a retail expert would evaluate the merits of items that a customer already owned but had stopped using or consigned to the attic. The personal shoppers would offer their rediscovery services in areas of fashion, furnishings, music and even food (recommending how an old tin of kidney beans could be put to use). The consultants would either charge a flat fee for their service or would sell back to the customer any long-lost items of monetary or sentimental value unearthed.

Dan Friedman
28 November 2001

324

Set up a subscription-based digital radio station that would play DJ sets tailored for use at private parties. The party host could select genres and request specific tracks in advance of the event and then simply tune into the set on the night.

Chas Bayfield
2 December 2001

Establish a company to sell advertising space on plaster casts, neck braces and slings. The medium might attract insurance companies or private healthcare operators. The advertising monies could be used to fund a patient's treatment and medication.

Sam Torme
5 December 2001

325

Editor's note:
Steven Qua definitely tapped into the zeitgeist with this idea. We were subsequently sent variations on this idea by numerous others, all of whom had probably suffered the embarrassment of accidentally, or rather too bravely, calling their parents at three o'clock in the morning.

Design a mobile phone with an in-built breathalyser that would bar the user from making potentially embarrassing or abusive calls to unfortunate friends and family when under the influence of alcohol. The phone could be programmed to allow drunken calls to, say, three numbers – taxi, police and pizza.

Steven Qua
7 December 2001

326

327

Create an Internet site for members of the public to upload drawings of people created from their imaginations. Once published, visitors to the site could look for themselves or for friends and upload actual photographs to prove the likenesses. Visitors who spotted an accidental representation would be able to purchase the original doodle – now an uncanny portrait – for a price that would compare favourably to that charged by professional portrait artists.

Charles Addison
8 December 2001

328

Encourage the public to exercise by introducing special signs to public parks, roadsides and other spaces offering distances from the sign to another given point. A sign might read '400 metres to the kid's swings', for example, and would also declare the world record for the specific distance. An automatic timer could be employed such that the runner hits the button on the sign and then again on the final point to see their own personal time.

Chas Bayfield
9 December 2001

Introduce a service in sports and shoe shops offering to 'break-in' footwear. A simple hygienic sock could be worn by the 'breaker inner' to protect from athlete's foot and the like. Customers could choose their 'degrees of wear' including normal wear and tear, football in the park or slam dancing. If the breaker inners were suitably fashionable, they would also be acting as a walking advertisement for the shoe while pounding the pavements.

Mat Fox
12 December 2001

Editor's note:
See also our cheap finger-printing kits idea for a means of settling disputes if this sticky dot innovation fails to take off.

Design small clips or sticky dots for pub drinkers to use in order to differentiate their glass from those of other customers. These distinctive personalised clips would be detachable so as to serve their purpose throughout an evening's drinking.

Tom Williams
17 December 2001

331

Design computer keyboards with words that are both regularly recurring and challenging to type printed under the standard QWERTY letters. A new function button could be used as a shift key to move from standard letter-by-letter typing to words. The words selected would be printed under appropriate letter keys, wherein the letter is the initial. 'Tomorrow' under 'T' or 'However' under 'H', for example.

Dave Jenner
19 December 2001

332

Open a food store selling only the very latest new product launches. Called Brand New Brands, the shop's stock would be completely untried and untested. Brands may even be persuaded to deliver stock without charge on the basis that their products would be promoted.

Charles Addison
20 December 2001

Editor's note:
Clearly the business of sending, reading and replying to email itself is not enough to keep the nation from actually doing any work.

Develop a game of email Frisbee. To play, an individual would enter the email address of a friend at a host website and, by controlling an on-screen avatar, would throw a Frisbee. The friend would then receive an email with an animated attachment showing a park and the sky above. At some point a Frisbee would enter the frame of the animation. The recipient would have to click on it before it hit the ground in order to catch it. The result would be recorded to a database as a catch or a drop. The recipient could then throw it back with a message or forward it to someone else. The team with the longest unbroken chain could be awarded a prize.

Chas Bayfield
21 December 2001

Design sunglasses that would lend the wearer the appearance of being permanently caught in a paparazzi-style photograph. The person's eyes would be deliberately obscured by a black rectangle, positioned slightly askew.

George Cockerill
22 December 2001

335

Release DVDs that offer the option of viewing a film with a lower certificate rating. By choosing this option, an alternative soundtrack without bad language would be heard and violent or sexually explicit scenes would be cut. This would enable young families or the overly sensitive to view popular adult films with greater confidence.

James Grainger
23 December 2001

Editor's note:
And no doubt the U-rated version of Reservoir Dogs could be watched from beginning to end in a fraction of the time needed for the original director's cut, thus saving time as well as blushes.

336

Design 'Autopause Headphones'. Whenever the listener lifted the headphones from their ears the music would stop playing and then resume when they were replaced.

Joe Gatt
25 December 2001

337

Design a multiplayer computer game in which each player is first tested physically and mentally before being assigned an access code for the game. The onscreen character would share the player's strength, height, IQ, weight, reaction times, disabilities, eyesight and age. Gamers would therefore have to improve themselves as much as their gaming skills to succeed in the game.

Tom Childs
26 December 2001

338

Sell hangover-treatment packs from vending machines in pubs and clubs. For a small sum, the packs could offer an aspirin or two, a sachet of coffee, aromatherapy oils and a fake doctor's note.

Tom Childs
27 December 2001

339

Launch a range of cocktail bubble-baths. These tonics would be coloured (and possibly flavoured) to replicate drinks such as Tequila Sunrise, Manhattan or Cement Mixer. Large sponges designed as lemon slices and cherries would be sold as accessories, along with inflatable ice-cube cushions for resting the head.

Mary Slim
2 January 2002

Editor's note:
Amazingly, this rather fun and gimmicky idea was misinterpreted when first published on Idea A Day. Some readers thought that we were suggesting a genuinely alcoholic and drinkable bath.

340

Manufacture greetings cards that can be programmed to develop over a period of time such that the image would only be fully seen on the intended date. These cards could be sent out before Christmas and, through the staggered release of chemical materials, develop gradually over the 12 festive days.

Dan Friedman
3 January 2002

341

Publish a hair and beauty magazine with hairstyles, jewellery and nail designs printed in actual size. These could be cut out and tried on by the reader to see whether they are suited to the designs.

Davey Moore
4 January 2002

342

Editor's note:
A telephone dial-up radio station might not be such bad idea in itself. Advertising revenues might cover the costs of providing a freephone number such that anyone with a phone could call up and listen in without charge.

Launch a radio station to broadcast over the telephone when customers are put on hold or in a call queue. The station could mix popular programming with interactive features, controlled by the users' touch-tone phones. Companies buying in to the service would receive discounted advertising on the station.

Danny Whitham
5 January 2002

343

Design an intelligent printer that wouldn't waste an entire sheet of paper printing out just a single widowed word, the arse-end of a disclaimer or the date and time on it. The printer would be able to make an educated guess as to whether the word or sentence should be included as a part of the document, and then rescale it to fit on a single page.

Iain Harrison
13 January 2002

344

Manufacture biros with flavoured tops to help writers to chew over ideas.

Rik Haslam
14 January 2002

Editor's note:
Charles Cohen objected to this idea: 'Pen chewing is a socially debilitating problem, particularly if one thoughtlessly chews a pen lent by a friend or colleague. Rather than providing a pleasant taste, the product should be foul tasting and cause the victim to gag on a pen end.

Create a scheme that makes use of the hours wasted spent holding in telephone queues for help desks and the like. When put on hold by companies subscribing to the scheme, the user's telephone number would be recognised by a centralised computer and a previously requested talking book, classic album or even language lesson would be broadcast. When the call was eventually answered the computer would bookmark the broadcast to be continued the next time the same caller was put on hold.

James Grainger
16 January 2002

Design special Christmas price stickers for children's presents such that stocking gifts given as if from Father Christmas would appear to have been bought in the 'Lapland General Store' rather than, for example, British Home Stores, thereby removing the pressure on aged relatives to remember to remove the labels.

Chas Bayfield
17 January 2002

347

Introduce a system for record stores which would print pertinent information at the bottom or on the back of till receipts. Information stating, for example, that a CD purchased was a band's second album or that the band were touring locally could be drawn from a central server.

Paul Scaife
18 January 2002

348

Reprogram Outlook, Hotmail and other email programmes such that they could scan outgoing email for any instance of the words 'attachment', 'enclosed' or 'please find'. If the user attempted to send such mail without an attachment, Outlook would ask, 'Did you mean to attach a document to this mail?'

George Cockerill
19 January 2002

Editor's note:
There must be a limit to how long the modern world can keep evolving without this idea being implemented.

349

Devise a range of sex toys and sexy underwear that incorporate infrared shutter-release triggers and remote controls for use in the creation of homemade pornography and erotica.

Sam Torme
22 January 2002

350

Devise an adult (or juvenile) mobile phone entertainment in which players are sent picture messages depicting bikini topped breasts and a unique code number. Each message would show only one of a pair. Players of the game must compare the bikini designs in search of a pair. When a pair was found, the players could reply to sender with their partner's code and would then be sent the pictures again — without the bikini top.

Dan Friedman
24 January 2002

351

Manufacture washing-up gloves with scour pads on the fingers and palms.

Mat Fox
26 January 2002

352

Devise a system that monitors live ratings for digital television and feeds back the information to individual viewers such that televisions can be programmed to recommend or automatically switch to the most popular programmes of the moment.

Justin Cooke
29 January 2002

Editor's note:
This could work now for websites and Internet traffic. Ultimately, users could set their preferences to notify them when, for example, any site more than trebled its average hits. No one need miss out on breaking news, dramatic shifts in share prices or newly published nude pictures of Drew Barrymore ever again.

353

Editor's note:
The staff would have to be on danger money, of course. Or paid in Vitamin C tablets.

Open a cafe bar called the Cold Room Club for anyone suffering from cold or flu symptoms but still able to get out of the house. At the club, customers could sit in an armchair or even lie in bed, order Lemsips and watch daytime television in the company of those similarly stricken.

Chas Bayfield
31 January 2002

354

Design bed linen with quilted or fleece-lined pockets at the bottom for sleepers to place their feet.

Angela Hill
1 February 2002

355

Manufacture a range of boxes that are deliberately designed to be extremely difficult to open. Whether encased in lead or reinforced plastic, the boxes would all contain a timer that would be triggered at the point of purchase. When a box was successfully opened, the owner would stop the timer and receive a unique code number, correlating directly to the time taken to open the box. The owner would then call a phone line with their code to claim a prize.

David Owen
2 February 2002

356

Design duvet covers with pornographic imagery printed on the underside.

Mike Hughes
3 February 2002

Editor's note:
Washing powder brands might benefit from giving these away for free to teenage boys.

357

Design ornate, coloured and unusually shaped and sized light bulbs for homeowners uncomfortable with a choice of chintzy lampshades or stark bare bulbs.

Becky Clarke
6 February 2002

358

Open a restaurant or café designed especially for pregnant women. Rather than a menu, the café would simply list the broadest possible choice of ingredients, including snow and sand and such like, from which customers could choose any combination to be prepared as they desired.

Sam Torme
9 February 2002

359

Open a restaurant offering famous and acclaimed dishes from great restaurants around the world. The meals would be prepared under license from the foreign chefs and chosen establishments. In addition to making wonderful cooking available to diners in their own country, the restaurant would act as an advertisement for the featured kitchens.

Charles Addison
10 February 2002

Editor's note:
And, like all good food ideas, this lends itself perfectly to the inevitable spin-off cookbook.

360

Design and distribute uniforms for members of the public who wish to be seen not only as upholding the law, but also as potential informers. These self-proclaimed snitches could wear T-shirts and caps declaring their intention to report any wrongdoings to the authorities and may actually deter many lawbreakers from operating in public.

David Owen
11 February 2002

361

Launch a radio station that continually broadcasts the last rites. Last Rites FM would be of immeasurable comfort to individuals finding themselves, or a loved one, close to death yet unable to call upon the services of a minister of religion. Persons of a more pessimistic nature would take comfort in knowing that, at one touch of a button, their pre-programmed car radio could receive Last Rites FM should an accident black spot or busy motorway take its toll.

Rupert Kaye
18 February 2002

362

Editor's note:
Of course, if a handle were attached to pick up another handle, and then another handle attached to lift them both, and so on, the whole thing would quickly become too heavy and cumbersome to lift at all.

Design a handle that could be attached by suction to heavy and/or oddly shaped objects. The personal grip would even be useful in carrying heavy bags that already have handles, in that it could be attached to the other side to balance the weight distribution or split the load between two people.

Mary Slim
23 February 2002

363

Publish a cartoon strip across the packaging of a number of associated products. Consumers could follow the fortunes of the characters on crisp packets, yoghurt pots and lollipop sticks. The familiarity of the comic strip would help introduce consumers to new products they might otherwise not try.

Charles Addison
24 February 2002

364

Produce a television commercial of typically striking, aspirational or quirky imagery, which doesn't actually name the advertiser. A competition would be run in which viewers could text or call in with their guesses as to what the ad might be trying to sell.

Dan Friedman
27 February 2002

Editor's note:
There are a great many television viewers who would fail this test of brand recognition even in response to commercials that do name the advertiser!

365

Create a series of cards that would be kept in wallets in case of accident or emergency. The cards would display a statement, such as 'Message to God: I don't go to church but I don't definitely disbelieve in you so please bear with me until I make up my mind'. The cards would be signed by the bearer and would offer those in a religious grey area some comfort that all might not be lost in the event of disaster.

Chas Bayfield
1 March 2002

366

Manufacture a transparent easel to allow amateur painters the chance to trace their subjects or landscapes. The painter would simply place the easel the correct distance from their subject to compose the picture. Clear sheets of textured plastic would provide a canvas to which paint would adhere.

Justin Hawkins
4 March 2002

367

Offer printed information-sheets at tube stations describing the advertising posters on display. Just as in a gallery, the written guides would offer information about the works, detailing the inspiration for each execution and, perhaps more usefully, an explanation of the message which the advertiser had hoped to deliver.

David Owen
6 March 2002

Editor's note:
We can make these disparaging jokes about advertising: some of our best friends are advertising creatives. Okay, all of our friends are advertising creatives!

368

Coordinate the computers in large offices such that the screensavers display signs to guide visitors around the building. If a party of foreign clients were visiting an office, the network of screensavers could be uploaded with directions to the toilets, meeting rooms and so on in the appropriate language.

Dan Friedman
7 March 2002

Manufacture His'n'Her blank video cassette packs in blue and pink. Following their introduction, there would be no excuse for one partner taping over the other's television favourites. Men may also find a certain appeal in openly maintaining a collection of blue movies.

Iain Harrison
9 March 2002

Design wall-mounted wooden cubes with hinges to all sides. In addition to providing storage space and a shelf, the cubes could also be folded out flat to the wall to serve as a decorative or symbolic cross for the Christian homeowner.

Charles Addison
10 March 2002

Editor's note: *Even without the religious symbolism of the cross (i.e. if the cupboard was not a cube and folded flat into more abstract shape), this has to be an IKEA product of the furture.*

321

Design door keys as distinct and attractive items fashioned from silver and gold such that they could double as earrings and pendants and always be at hand.

Mary Slim
11 March 2002

322

Design shoes that count each footstep taken when worn. Shoe designers could offer a free pair to anyone who records more than one million steps in the shoes. The competition could be made particularly exciting if the prize was only to be given to anyone clocking the total number of steps exactly on arrival back at the store.

Dan Friedman
16 March 2002

Award 'Benefit of the doubt' cards to motorists who maintain clean driving licenses for a number of years. Once displayed in the windscreen, the cards would effectively grant the driver an extra few minutes when illegally parked or an extra inch over a yellow line.

David Owen
18 March 2002

Editor's note:
We also remember a spin-off idea for a topless carwash service that used the strapline, 'I'll wash if you swipe'.

Design credit card reader-strips that can be adhered to any surface, including skin. Lap dancers could wear the reader in their bust, for example, to encourage frequent card swiping.

Mary Slim
20 March 2002

325

Licence the interior designs of the world's best hotel rooms for domestic refits. Any room of a great enough size could be redecorated and furnished exactly in the style of a suite at Claridges or a room at the Hotel Du Cap, for example.

Sven Larkson
25 March 2002

326

Counteract the negative connotations of graffiti in an urban area by spraying positive factual information such as numbers of local nursery places or directions to healthcare centres in the same graffiti style alongside or over existing daubs.

Dan Friedman
2 April 2002

377

Design a 'kinetic keyboard' for laptop computers. The battery life of the computer would be extended by the energy provided by the user's keystrokes when typing. When switched to 'kinetic mode' the keys would offer more resistance in order to convert more energy. The effort required would be similar to that needed when typing on an old fashioned manual typewriter.

Chas Bayfield
15 April 2002

378

Retail individual, bottled fizzy drinks with plastic drinking straws already inside the bottles. When the cap is unscrewed, the straw would be lifted above the neck by the air bubbles.

Dan Friedman
17 April 2002

Redesign standard food packaging to include a secret compartment. In a packet of biscuits the hidden compartment could contain a few more biscuits so that the last ones were as fresh as the first. The compartments could also be used to include a sample of another product. A packet of Cornflakes might contain a bonus serving of a newly launched cereal, which would be introduced just at the point when the consumer ran out of the main product.

David Owen
18 April 2002

Editor's note:
The latest updates on
www.idea-a-day.com
might act in much the
same way for readers
of this book.

Devise an online 'listening booth' to preview new music. The booth would only be operative if more than one listener were logged in on each channel at the same time. In effect, this would mean that a fan of a band would need to persuade someone else to log on so they could hear a new track.

Sam Torme
23 April 2002

381

Design a bicycle with a lock built into the frame. An integral section of the frame could be removed and locked back so that the frame itself acted effectively as the lock.

Chas Bayfield
1 May 2002

382

Editor's note:
A Wayne Hemingway favourite. Wayne has a fish tank cistern in his downstairs loo so he recognises a good toilet innovation idea when he sees one.

Design a lavatory cistern with a sink bowl in the lid. When flushed, the clean water filling the cistern could be used for handwashing.

Julian Richardson
2 May 2002

383

Design labels made from blotting paper to wrap completely around the neck or body of wine bottles. The labels would soak up any drips of wine before they reached the tablecloth.

Jim Bolton
3 May 2002

384

Design binocular/spectacles with a focal range of around one metre for train and underground commuters keen to read the newspapers and magazines of their fellow passengers. The lenses could be set in such a way that the wearer would appear to be looking in a slightly different direction so as to avoid conflict.

Sam Torme
9 May 2002

Editor's note:
Yes, this is obviously a stupid idea but not as stupid as a horizontal periscope for reading over other people's shoulders, which we declined to publish.

385

Launch a new snack food range called 'Forkfuls'. The products would comprise frozen mouthfuls of foodstuffs such as steak and kidney pie or lasagne with forks already inserted into them. The forks would be inexpensive and microwave proof such that the snacks could be taken directly from the freezer, heated up and eaten.

Chas Bayfield
14 May 2002

386

Editor's note:
Following on from the astounding 'Forkfuls', we surprised ourselves with this social and political idea. It does actually seem to be both well intentioned and workable.

Offer any young person due to turn 18 during the term of an elected government the opportunity to vote on their birthday. Although their vote would not technically make a difference it could be reported on a website and would reflect the prevailing mood of a country's youth on any given day. The birthday poll would also focus young people on political issues and remind them of the power now vested in them.

David Owen
17 May 2002

387

Design a range of keys with a clear plastic window in the grip part of the key. If the key were used to lock a door a red tag would automatically pop into view by means of a simple spring mechanism. Similarly, a green tag or one with 'Unlocked' printed on it would be visible when the door was unlocked.

Andrew Hussey
21 May 2002

388

Launch a chocolate bar, or other such simple product, with a promise to the public that the bar would never change its name, branding or size (even the price could be tied to inflation). Over the years, the product would come to symbolise stability, honesty and permanence – all very attractive brand values – while offering a somewhat critical angle from which to consider the fickle nature of commercialism exhibited by competing products.

Dan Friedman
27 May 2002

Editor's note:
*Toby Gunton pointed
out the ironic potential
for this idea to be
rolled out to other
businesses; pubs for
teetotallers, brothels
for the celibate.*

Start a dance club at which people would be asked to leave if they danced too well. In addition to attracting normally shy and clumsy types onto the dance floor, the club might well attract great natural dancers for whom disguising such ability could become a whole new craze.

Zoot
31 May 2002

389

Design an intruder alarm that, some minutes after initially sounding off, would start up again with the pre-recorded sound of an approaching police car.

Mary Slim
12 June 2002

390

391

Design fish tank crèches at the heart of new workspaces. Staff could leave their children at these subsidised, secure areas under the supervision of qualified minders. Employers would enjoy increased workplace morale, while sound-proofing would allow employees to enjoy just the sight of children playing as they worked.

Liam Donnelly
26 June 2002

392

Introduce telephone boxes that lock from the inside. Individuals under threat of street crime or violence could lock themselves away from harm and call for help. If built from bullet-proof glass, anyone sheltering inside would be safe from harm and openly in view of passers-by or the police. The transparency would also discourage any inappropriate use of the booths.

Charles Addison
27 June 2002

393

Design inflatable swimming costumes. Such items could complement or replace armbands and floats for learners. They could also inflate the egos of men or women who might otherwise be a little self-conscious wearing such skimpy outfits at the pool or beach.

Sam Torme
29 June 2002

394

Provide a service in supermarkets whereby staff would loosen or undo packaging such as jars and sealed plastic lids on juice cartons for elderly or disabled customers.

Chas Bayfield
8 July 2002

395

Establish a chain of 'anti-fashion' stores, which would monitor the colours and styles chosen by the main retailers for the season and deliberately set out to sell goods outside the boundaries set by fashion, thus increasing consumer choice.

Gerard Johnson
24 July 2002

Editor's note:
Quite a number of those who reviewed these ideas before publication made the point that these stores already exist. They are called C&A.

396

Introduce a system of 'survival' tokens in varying denominations, which the public could purchase from high street stores and give to the homeless in preference to cash. The tokens could be exchanged for food, clothing and non-alcoholic drinks.

Stuart McGlashan
23 August 2002

Editor's note:
We make no claim for the originality of this idea. While running Idea A Day, the same idea was submitted by different people at least ten times. If not new, it certainly has some validity.

397

Add a button to digital television remote-controls that would flash to alert viewers as to when an ad break has ended on the channel they were watching. A sonic alarm would be useful for viewers who leave the room while the commercials play out, while a flashing light would be sufficient to alert those who prefer to channel hop.

Jeremy Conrad
18 September 2002

398

Invite the many investment bankers, accountants and lawyers who are made redundant during periods of recession to brainstorm Next Generation solutions for health, transport and other public service industries. When the professionals find new employment, they could be rewarded for their charitable contributions by way of a tax-break on the first six months of their new income.

idletimes
30 September 2002

399

Develop a shopping ID card that could be swiped at the till, allowing stores to email a receipt rather than print one. This would save paper, as most receipts are discarded, and would ensure a record of purchase is kept securely. Email receipts could upload directly to spreadsheets for business customers.

James Hamilton
2 October 2002

400

Launch a company called Second Skin to trade in used tattoos. The tattoos would be acquired from dead people who had bequeathed their skin, or by living donors in desperate need of money. Customers would choose designs to be grafted onto their own bodies. Antique, or vintage celebrity tattoos could become the next fashion must-have.

David Owen
4 October 2002

Editor's note:
There is a classic film called 'The Hands of Dr Orlac' in which a concert pianist loses his hands in an accident and a surgeon (played by Peter Lorre) replaces them with the hands of a recently hung serial killer. That didn't turn out too well though.

401

Introduce a new form of marriage. Contracts could be negotiated to last five, ten or fifteen years. Or they could be structured like record deals; for two children, with options to follow.

Peer Fischer
11 October 2002

402

Editor's note:
Such a 'Homes Reunited' site has now been launched. There was also another idea for an online wallpaper matching service that would work well in tandem with this one.

Launch a website where people can submit photographs of themselves, their friends, family or pets, in houses, apartments, and other places they have lived. They would also submit the address of the place where the photo was taken. Other people could then log on and see how their current home used to look when people they have never met were living there.

Casey Morello
13 October 2002

403

Create tattoo ink that would be visible only under ultraviolet light, thereby allowing people to show off their body art in clubs but keep it hidden during the day.

Marc John Weeks
23 October 2002

Editor's note:
Such nocturnal revelations might also come as quite a surprise to the convent school girl who realises too late that she has brought one of Motley Crue home to meet her parents.

404

Create a centralised online reference library of instruction manuals for discontinued electrical, mechanical and other technical goods.

Antony Hart
31 October 2002

405

Incorporate speakers into statues. At the press of a button, a voice would explain who the figure was, what they achieved, who created the statue and why it was situated in a particular location.

Chas Bayfield
14 December 2002

406

Launch a website called iwasright.com at which anyone involved in an argument or dispute, which could not be immediately resolved, could securely post and date-stamp their answer for verification at a later date. If proved right, the individual could request the site to send a smug and official email to whomever got it wrong.

David Owen
15 December 2002

407

Introduce a new mobile phone service that would allow users to 'ping' each other and receive information as to the whereabouts, present company, or mood of their friends when their phones are switched off, without actually disturbing them. Users would input the information they wished to provide in the auto response texts: 'awake' or 'asleep', 'bored and lonely', 'kidnapped but unharmed' and so on.

Dan Friedman
16 December 2002

Editor's note:
If mobile phones continue to become smaller and more advanced at an equal rate we may well have virtual telepathy before this book hits a second edition.

408

Place a specially constructed rubber balloon in the hull of oil tankers to be filled with crude oil, and use the normal hull for ballast water. The ballast seawater would not create pollution when dumped into the sea and, should an accident occur, the rubber balloon would hold the crude oil and prevent an oil spill.

Dr Hamad Alsaad
17 December 2002

Develop a crash helmet with a self-cleaning visor. The visor would be shaped so that it wrapped right around the circumference of the helmet. It would rotate at the press of a button and pass under squeegees at either side, which would clean it and wipe away excess water.

Jim Richards
18 December 2002

Install digital cameras to the changing rooms of clothes shops. Using MMS picture messaging technology, customers could send a picture of themselves in their prospective outfit to a friend to solicit their opinion.

Andrew Pearce
20 December 2002

411

Publish a series of 'Genius Guides', parodying the typical 'Idiots Guides'. The books would instruct the very clever reader in how to undertake simple tasks such as wiring a plug, boiling an egg, or sitting through church services and episodes of soap operas without making cynical remarks.

David Owen
24 December 2002

412

Design recyclable Christmas and greetings cards. The cards would have a number of blank inserts stuck inside on which the sender could write a message. Once the festivities were over the recipients could peel off the message, rewrite and resend the card – preferably not to the original sender.

Mary Slim
25 December 2002

Editor's note:
Alternatively, the use of pencils and erasers could be encouraged through a national advertising campaign that sought to readdress the status held by pen and ink.

413

Add an extra page to the back of library books on which borrowers could leave notes for the next reader. In addition to simply passing on their critical thoughts or leaving recommendations for further reading, borrowers may like to leave contact details in order to meet like-minded readers for fun, friendship and maybe more.

Charles Addison
26 December 2002

414

Conduct a consumer-research programme based on children's Christmas lists. The letters to Father Christmas could be posted care of a newspaper or magazine, which could then determine the most popular gifts of the season. By publishing the top 100 Most Wanted presents in advance, stores could prepare themselves for the demand and offer parents further inspiration before Christmas shopping.

Mary Slim
28 December 2002

Improve the ordering procedure at fast food restaurants, drive-thrus and other service centres where the average IQ of the customer is likely to be equal to, or greater than, that of the staff, by offering the customer their own keypad and access to the onscreen system. Customers could make and confirm their own selections while staff would be freed up to concentrate on preparing food, cleaning and smiling.

T B Prickett
29 December 2002

Editor's note:
The Big Idea Book partners Chas Bayfield and Rupert Kaye have both worked for McDonalds – Rupert as a restaurant manager. Both tried to quash this idea on the grounds that it was unfair to belittle the mental prowess of such employees. Of course, they lacked the intellectual rigour to win the ensuing argument.

Publish a book of begging letters. Members of the public would be invited to submit their pleas in the most eloquent terms and the most dramatic/amusing would be published. The authors would waive any royalty from sales of the book but would be given a PO Box number at which they may or may not receive handouts.

Dan Friedman
30 December 2002

Upload a web page on which a well-known piece of writing is published: a chapter from a classic novel, the transcript of a political speech or a newspaper report, perhaps. Editing tools would be offered on the site, allowing readers to rewrite the piece – amending, adding or deleting as they saw fit. Subsequent visitors to the site would see only the hijacked version but would be able to continue altering the words and meaning or even correcting the text if they were so incensed. At random points, the pieces would be saved and archived and replaced by new extracts.

David Owen
31 December 2002

Launch a chain of 'cab and kebab' shops. Late night revellers would be assured a cab in the time they have eaten a kebab, burger or other fast food snack of their choice.

James Hamilton
1 January 2003

Design wall plaques in the general style of English Heritage's Blue Plaques. Rather than commemorating famous and worthy individuals that may once have lived in a building, the new plaques would simply declare the name of the current residents in the most ostentatious fashion.

Sam Torme
5 January 2003

Design a line of underwear with messages like 'I'm thinking of someone else', 'Only in it for the sex' and 'I'll be gone before you wake up' printed on them. The range would be marketed under the brand name of Freudian Slips.

Stuart McGlashan
9 January 2003

Editor's note:
One of the few examples in which the idea is just as good as the pun that inspired it.

421

Assign a different colour to each day of a week on a global basis. Travellers could quickly recognise days of the week on timetables and displays without having to read the language. The universal colour coding could also be used in the design of pill cases, diaries and calendars.

Myatmo
10 January 2003

422

Editor's note:
A version of 'Wife Swap' in which bands play gigs with the singer from another group might also prove popular. Fran Healy of Travis standing in for one of Blue, for example.

Produce a fly on the wall documentary series called 'House Bands' in which two very different rock or pop acts would agree to live together for a month or two in a shared house. Earth Wind and Fire might take in Leonard Cohen as a lodger, for example.

Charles Addison
17 January 2003

423

Design a memory-loss drug (a mild variation on Rohypnol perhaps) for parents to administer to children at their discretion. A child prone to copycat behaviour such as repeating swear words when overheard could be given a swift dose when such an incident occurs in the hope that they would forget all about it.

Dan Friedman
20 January 2003

424

Launch an Internet wastebasket into which members of the public can upload files that they wish to delete from their own computers and servers but that they think may possibly have some use or value to others. A credit system could be introduced where, for each megabyte of original files dumped on the site, the sender is awarded a minute of access to forage for themselves in the rubbish tip.

David Owen
22 January 2003

Editor's note:
With a smart search engine attached, the unwanted data could become genuinely useful. How many people, for example, call Directory Enquiries for telephone numbers which hundreds of other people already know?

425

Design milk cartons with a litmus strip that changes colour depending on the freshness of the milk. A face could be printed over the strip – turning green when the milk is off.

Russell Tucker
28 January 2003

426

Design a pair of car stereo speakers in the shape of two dogs' heads. As a relatively high tech update of the classic nodding dogs found in the rear window of many cars, the 'woofer' speakers could also be programmed to nod along in time with the music being played.

David Owen
29 January 2003

427

Introduce an emergency short code for SMS text. Anyone in trouble but unable to talk could text messages to a number such as 11999. The shortcode could also be used to send MMS images of accidents or crimes.

Justin Cooke
31 January 2003

428

Introduce a tax to be paid by all companies that advertise products and services, which would be collected and redistributed by the government to fund advertising for alternative lifestyle choices that cost nothing to follow and are therefore of no interest to industry. Commercials espousing the benefits of going barefoot, wearing plaits or picking blackberries would contrast nicely with the typical adverts for cars, credit cards and building societies.

David Owen
3 February 2003

Editor's note:
Such commercials would also save The Green Party from ever having to fund their own party political activities again!

429

Produce dolls that, in appearance and actual size, are intended to represent children older than those who will own them. The older dolls may not be able to care for their owners but they could be programmed to say things like, 'Jeez, why don't you leave me alone?' or 'What's wrong with your own friends?'

Charles Addison
10 February 2003

430

Editor's note:
There was also an idea submitted to leaflet-drop such tricky trivia questions to two warring nations giving one side the answers to the other's questions and vice-versa.

Publish a book of fiendishly difficult quiz questions and distribute it for free. None of the answers would be published in the book. Instead a premium-rate phone line or paid-for SMS text service would be advertised by which readers could ascertain the correct answers.

Sam Torme
11 February 2003

Create a subscription TV channel called Sub-SubTitles. The programmes broadcast would be reruns of old television favourites or syndicated news programmes. The channel would write its own subtitles to improve, subvert or otherwise change the viewing experience. For example, the news could be sub-subtitled with a series of factual statements that might contradict or endorse the reporting. Soap operas could be enlivened with a lighter 'subtext' to the dialogue. Satire could be added to topical debates and humour added to otherwise bland programming.

Jim Richards
20 February 2003

Design discreet earphones as decorative earrings.

Liam Donnelly
23 February 2003

433

Allow people with large debts to supplement whatever cash payment they can afford to make with work for their community.

Julian Richardson
3 March 2003

434

Launch a premium-rate phone line on which callers who have returned from abroad or simply risen late in the day can speak to an informed call-centre operator and ask any questions they like about the weather, sports results, likelihood of war and so on.

David Owen
19 March 2003

435

Launch a temporary communal credit card account or Kitty Card for groups of people who are going on vacation together. The card would have an agreed credit limit, each person in the group would be a signatory, and each would be billed equally at the end of the agreed period.

Chas Bayfield
27 March 2003

436

Open a shop in which everything is free. Every trial pack of shampoo or perfume tester available in magazines and other promotions would be presented on mass in the store. The shop would become a focus point for market research, an ideal location for new product launches, and, as such, could be funded by the companies benefiting from the exposure.

Sam Torme
17 April 2003

Editor's note:
The shop would also, as Wayne Hemingway pointed out to us, provide excellent therapy for compulsive shoplifters.

437

Develop a website for groups of people to request tenders for services. For example, the residents of a particular street could make deals to insure all their houses or cars together.

Julian Richardson
22 April 2003

438

Editor's note:
Surely a range of
T-shirts bearing the
original naff bumper
stickers such as 'My
other car is a Porsche'
would clean up as
ironic retro wear for
students. 'My other
shirt's in the wash'
might also work.

Design a range of post-ironic, self-referencing retro products such as red rectangular bumper-stickers for cars with white poster-style italic letters declaring 'These bumper stickers used to be really popular in the late 80s', or outsize white T-shirts with block, black lettering declaring 'These T-shirts used to make fashion and political statements'.

Dan Friedman
20 April 2003

439

Develop an Invisible Graffiti application for mobile phones. Utilising GPS, any adolescent struck with either an amusing observation about a building, or the desperate urge to tag their whereabouts, would be encouraged to commit their thoughts to text message (or a simple paint package on an image phone). Any other young person with the application running on their phone would be sent the message or daubing as they passed the same location at a later date.

Dan Friedman
25 April 2003

Editor's note:
Wayne Hemingway was particularly unimpressed by this idea: 'No wonder there was a dot com crash. Ideas like this affected my pension.'

440

Publish meeting places on a daily basis in national or local newspapers. Whether a park bench, a coffee shop or a gallery, the places would provide the lonely or curious with somewhere to go where they would be likely to meet other people at an equally loose end. Conversation at these designated rendezvous points would be relatively easy to strike up as those present could always start with something like, 'Did you read about this in...?' If popular, the newspapers could charge a fee to cafés, theatres, galleries and the like for their selection on a particular day.

David Owen
26 April 2003

Editor's note:
There is an underground/Internet movement that is sometimes referred to as 'swarming' that works in a similar fashion. This was responsible for an unfeasibly large crowd of strangers arriving on mass at a branch of DFS somewhere in the country.

441

Design car headlights that automatically flash whenever a driver sounds their horn. In heavy traffic, the lights would help identify exactly which driver was expressing their frustration.

Martyn Jones
2 May 2003

442

Promote the use of bicycles in congested city areas by introducing a special quota of stools in bars and cafés reserved for cyclists. Offering up a sharp, vertical metal pole rather than a seat, the stools would require the placement of a cycle saddle on the top to offer any comfort whatsoever.

Mary Slim
4 May 2003

Develop a range of flavoured lipsticks to be worn by women but targeted at men. They would come in suitably bloke-friendly flavours such as beer, curry sauce or salt 'n' vinegar and would be called Licksticks.

Trevor Webb
8 May 2003

Editor's note:
If Trevor Web could see just one of his ideas realised, we are guessing this would be his first choice.

Design a range of T-shirts for women that lend the wearer the appearance of a larger bust. Typical slogans or designs would be stretched over a generously proportioned tailor's dummy before being photographed and reapplied to shirts of a standard size.

Dan Friedman
12 May 2003

Editor's note:
And, of course, we should like to take this opportunity to thank everyone who ever submitted an idea to Idea A Day, whether it made it into this book or not. And our editor at Wiley-Capstone, our web designer, the manager of the local...

445

Launch a website on which members of the public could officially say thank you to family, friends or colleagues who had helped them in completing a particular project. The site's permanent registry would represent the ordinary person's version of album sleeve notes, film credits or Oscar acceptance speeches.

David Owen
14 May 2003

446

Design trousers with towelling pocket linings for businessmen of nervous dispositions and sweaty palms.

James Hamilton
17 May 2003

447

Design a device in the form of a glove or a sensor that could record the unique qualities of a handshake. The device would register the strength of a squeeze, the size of the hand and the vigour employed in shaking. The properties of celebrity handshakes could be recorded and published such that members of the public could collect shakes like autographs.

David Owen
23 May 2003

Editor's note:
If this took off, celebrities could well be first in the queue for James Hamilton's trousers from the previous page.

448

Manufacture black plastic bin liners impregnated with a substance known to deter rats such as rapeseed oil. The pest-controlling refuse sacks would be marketed as RatBags.

Trevor Webb
29 May 2003

Editor's note:
By now, the reader should be in no doubt whatsoever that Trevor Webb does indeed think of the names of his innovations before assigning them a function.

449

Launch a number of online shops carrying items retailing at specific values such as £5, £10 or greater. Shoppers with a present to buy and a specific budget, or online shoppers with a small Paypal balance at their disposal, could type in the appropriate URL (twentypoundstospend.co.uk) and be presented with a range of choices including books, CDs, clothes and such like.

David Owen
1 June 2003

450

Develop an application for standard electronic diaries with which the public could decide whether they had had a good or a bad day. A scale of one to ten could be used with space provided for personal comments such as 'I fell in love' or 'I had diarrhoea'. The individual scores could be collated and published in a newspaper alongside the weather forecast and pollen count as an indication of the nation's prevailing mood.

3 June 2003
Sergei Ivanov

454

Organise stalking tours of major cities. Groups of interested people would meet at a given start point, and then simply follow a local home. Once the passer-by had arrived home or at work, a new tour would begin. The tours would provide an unusual way of getting to know a city.

Dushawn Jackson
4 June 2003

452

Design a wristwatch that digitally counts down to the end of the wearer's life. Given that the average life expectancy for a male is 74 years, or 650,000 hours, a 34-year-old would have 322,560 hours of life remaining. Once the wearer enters in their present age the watch would beep as every hour passed to their eventual estimated demise. The watch would be called the DeathWatch.

Trevor Webb
16 June 2003

453

Launch a book-reading club through online retailers such as Amazon. Books offered for sale could be tagged by individuals who were either currently reading them, or waiting to read them when others were ready to share the experience.

Dan Friedman
20 June 2003

454

Editor's note:
Customers could also consider donating items they had bought as an investment – functional antiques such as vases or lamps, for example – to the disadvantaged to use while they appreciate in value.

Launch a new retail concept which invites customers to purchase items but also to donate them to someone else for a designated period of time. Customers may wish to pay for a tennis racquet, for example, that would be given to a new talent in the sport to use before being returned to the purchaser. The player would have their equipment paid for and the customer would have a perfectly good racquet that had been used by a potential Wimbledon champion.

David Owen
21 June 2003

454

Publish an introductory reader book, which would present the first chapters of a number of forthcoming novels. The book would retail at a typical paperback price but the customer's receipt could be retained as proof of purchase and used as a voucher to gain money off any of the titles previewed in the sample volume.

Dan Friedman
25 June 2003

455

Devise an Internet and email application for people to make and record predictions. Participants would enter the email addresses of whomever they would like notified of any predictions they make. The emails would not be sent, however, until either the guessed at event or outcome had occurred, or the time specified in the prediction had elapsed. If the prediction proved to be inaccurate there would be nothing the individual could do to stop the application from sending their failed projection to all the friends whom they had hoped impress.

David Owen
27 June 2003

Editor's note:
In the spirit of this idea, we assert that The Big Idea Book will hit the bestseller lists. This prediction will of course look particularly unimpressive if this page is being read in a remainder bookshop.

457

Manufacture a toilet block which changes colour when urinated on. The block could be used to monitor abnormalities in diet, detect pregnancies or drug test visitors.

Simon
30 June 2003

458

Design an Auto Butt – a device that would collect rainwater falling on cars and channel it into the windscreen-wash bottle or even store it as a reserve supply for the radiator.

Jack Dolan
1 July 2003

459

Introduce a new character to written English which would be a question mark with a comma rather than a full stop at the bottom, thereby allowing writers to pose questions within sentences, such as, 'Is this a good idea?, I think so.'

Jan Van Mesdag
30 June 2003

460

Launch a range of electric wheelchairs for able-bodied people. Designed for the 'Slacker' market they would enable people to go shopping, or out for drinks, without having to go to the trouble of getting out of their seat.

Trevor Webb
5 July 2003

Editor's note:
Although pictures of Chloe Sevigny or Spike Jonze rolling up to the Oscars in a designer wheelchair might make disability cool, we can't imagine genuinely disabled people thinking that this is a very good idea. Besides, it never took off for Clive Sinclair.

461

Use the heat from a vehicle's exhaust manifold to heat screen-wash water for de-icing in winter and better cleaning in summer.

Julian Richardson
6 July 2003

462

Design contact lenses that would glow under ultra-violet light. UV torches would be sold to wearers for use in the event of loss. The glow-in-the-dark lenses might also prove popular with night clubbers.

Sander De Jong
7 July 2003

463

Design a novelty, talking mirror, which would be pre-programmed to offer random fashion and diet tips, such as 'Go back to bed!' or 'Looks like you've lost weight'. The mirror would be just as accurate or inaccurate in its statements as the Magic 8 ball but possibly just as popular.

Chas Bayfield
8 July 2003

Editor's note:
Sometimes we get the feeling that we would have been better off by simply publishing an extra edition of the Innovations Catalogue than this book – and thereby cut out out the middleman.

464

Introduce standard labelling for food products that change colour (probably always to green) when the product reaches its sell-by date. Foodstuffs that do actually change colour when out of date need only be packed in clear containers.

Alex Hawkins
10 July 2003

Display vehicle velocity in metres per second as well as mph/kph to provide drivers with an idea of speed and stopping distances that can be more easily visualised.

Ant Evans
12 July 2003

Editor's note:
Toby Gunton suggested that it may well be more interesting to introduce real news stories into soaps rather than the other way round. Did September 11th have any impact on Eastenders?

Publish a weekly local newspaper covering the fictional areas in which a popular television soap opera is set. The paper would develop its own news stories, which would only involve characters from the programme when a storyline was sufficiently newsworthy (murder, arson etc), or if it were thought likely that a character might win a crossword competition or a beauty contest. The paper would be sold nationally and carry real advertising alongside its fictional editorial.

David Owen
15 July 2003

467

Design drivers' seats for three-door cars that lock into their forward positions when parked to deter car thieves and joyriders or at least make their getaways very uncomfortable.

Phil Tredinnick
17 July 2003

468

Launch a new product using a marketing strategy called Siamese Marketing. The product would be given two different brand names and each would have separate advertising campaigns. Brand 'A' would be advertised in a deliberately offensive fashion, and would be 'The Sickly Brand'. Brand 'B' would feed off the bad publicity of its twin and slowly build its own customer base to grow into being 'The Healthy Brand'. Eventually 'The Sickly Brand' would die leaving only healthy brand.

Editor's note:
A great idea in principle but it has surely been undermined already by the actual success of the ultimate 'sickly brand', Tango.

Trevor Webb
18 July 2003

Produce a nightly terrestrial television programme comprising the highlights (or lowlights) from the day's daytime output. The review programme would be broadcast in the evening to appeal to anyone in employment who would have been unavailable or disinclined to sit through seven hours of chat shows and makeovers. It would probably work in the same fashion as the outtakes shown at the end of some films.

Sam Torme
22 July 2003

Editor's note:
Although employers would never condone such a scheme, it is not so far removed in principle from corporate moves to outsource local call centres, for example, to India and the Far East.

Launch a discreet service that would undertake short-term professional contract work anonymously on behalf of those who need a little help to get their jobs done. Akin to essay writing services for students, the programme would let people continue to cheat after they enter the work place, should an assignment prove too difficult or should the worker just fall too far behind.

Barbara
23 July 2003

471

Introduce a secular godparenting service called Oddparents, which would provide a diverse and unconventional range of mentors to children.

Adam Atkinson
25 July 2003

472

Include the numbers for local services and businesses, such as those for takeaways and cab companies, in the address books of newly purchased mobile phones.

Becky Clarke
28 July 2003

Editor's note:
There must also be a case for a directory enquiries by text service. Presumably, it is only the greater profits generated from voice calls to 118 numbers that have deterred any telecommunications company from introducing such a system.

423

Introduce a system for newly-built flats and housing developments wherein one flat or property would be left unsold and owned on a timeshare basis by all the new residents. The surplus flat would typically be booked out for visiting guests but could also prove invaluable for residents as an alternative to sleeping on sofas following domestic arguments or, in the instance of double bookings by estranged partners, the perfect place to conduct an affair.

Mary Slim
3 August 2003

424

Create edible candles from sugar paste, honey or some other such foodstuff that approximates candle wax. Enthusiastic children could blow out the flames, have their cake and eat the candles, while those of little puff can at least still eat the cake when the candles have completely melted over the icing.

Sven Keitel
7 August 2003

Offer premium-rate billing to domestic telephone customers. Homeowners could set a rate at which calls to their number would be charged. The monies earned would be set against the user's own phone bill. Users could pre-select rates for all, or just specific, incoming calls. Rather than barring calls from a persistent telesales company, for example, the user would simply select an expensive tariff to deter them. Calls placed to numbers operating the system would be greeted with a message outlining the call charges and allowing the caller time to hang up if they would rather not pay.

David Owen
7 August 2003

Editor's note:
This would also appeal to those who would love to attend a famous school but would never want to board there.

Establish franchises or chains of famous public schools and universities. Outposts of the Cheltenham Ladies College or Kings College, Cambridge could be opened across the country and throughout the world. Existing local schools and colleges could be acquired, rebranded and the staff retrained by experienced teachers from the original establishments.

Dan Friedman
11 August 2003

477

Design a range of bicycles under the brand name of Recycles. The bikes could be fashioned from decommissioned weapons and tanks. The redeployment of such materials would appeal equally to right-on parents and their gun crazy kids, albeit for quite different reasons.

Jim Bolton
12 August 2003

478

Introduce an offer of free tattoos in any style or design for anyone willing to have an equally sized permanent tattoo of a major brand-name logo etched onto their skin at the same time. Brands such as Nike or Ralph Lauren could fund the offer through local tattoo parlours.

Rufus Redstone
13 August 2003

429

Open a golf course that is also a cemetery. Golfers reaching retirement age would be welcome to join and play regularly – safe in the knowledge that their green fees and membership subscriptions would be contributing to the upkeep of their eventual resting place. Members wishing to be buried could choose a plot adjacent to their favourite fairway, while those preferring to be cremated could request their ashes to be scattered over any number of bunkers.

Pat Nichols
14 August 2003

Editor's note:
If nothing else, this idea would lend the world at least a hundred new jokes. Dead balls, awkward lies – the possibilities are endless.

430

Open a theme park called Weatherland at which visitors would be subjected to all manners of 'artificially conjured' natural events, including tornados, monsoons, heatwaves and blizzards. Visitors who normally enjoy getting soaked on log flumes would literally be in their element, while others could relax on the beach.

Charles Addison
18 August 2003

481

Introduce a system to airports in which the newspapers and magazines left behind on planes by passengers arriving from long-haul destinations would be collected and resold locally or distributed to passengers flying out from the terminal.

Justin Cooke
19 August 2003

482

Editor's note:
Being so close to the end of the book, the comment on this page corner would be a plug for The Big Idea Book II – watch this space.

Print messages upside down and in small text in the top corners of book pages. If a reader folded a corner down as a bookmark, they would see the message. Early pages of a book, for example, could be annotated with phrases such as, 'Oh c'mon. Five more pages, please. Give it a chance.'

David Owen
20 August 2003

483

Implement an additional feature to home videogame consoles that would allow for more than one television to be connected. Households with two or more televisions could enjoy multiplayer games, with each player having their own screen and view on the action.

Stefan Morris
21 August 2003

484

Redesign the rear passenger windows of family cars such that children travelling in the back could draw on the windows. The glass could be wiped clean and each picture erased when the window was wound down. Children could also colour in the whole window to provide themselves with a sunscreen.

Dan Friedman
22 August 2003

485

Editor's note:
Davey Moore submitted another similar concept at the same time, wherein breakfast radio shows would deliver such positive statements at set intervals such that individuals could set radio alarm clocks to wake them to the messages.

Manufacture an alarm clock called a Salaam clock. The Salaam clock would be programmed with a selection of self-help aphorisms, good tidings and confidence-boosting messages. These affirmative statements would be randomly selected to wake people up and help them start the day with something other than an inhuman beep, buzz, chime or inane radio chat.

Davey Moore
24 August 2003

486

Redesign toilet rolls such that the cylinder in the middle would be made from a substance that dissolves in water. The tube could then be thrown away down the toilet when the roll was finished.

Dave Jenner
26 August 2003

487

Create Star Glasses, which show the names and positions of all of the constellations to the wearer. Simply by aligning a dot on the glasses to the North star, the wearer would be able to move his or her head until the stars in the sky are aligned with the map and information printed on the inside of the glasses. Different Star Glasses would be available for different times in different parts of the world.

Mike Ward
27 August 2003

488

Introduce a system by which music fans would be rewarded with discounts or complimentary albums for playing their favourite songs on pub and club jukeboxes. Customers would enter a unique pin before making their track selections with each play for a particular artist adding a point to their personal account. In effect, fans would be able to buy a forthcoming album by their favourite act by repeatedly playing the artist's music in public.

David Owen
28 August 2003

Introduce 'address for life' code numbers to everyone in the country. People could register their current address with the post office such that letters addressed with the code number would be forwarded from the sorting office. In addition to offering everyone PO Box-style privacy, the system would come into its own when people moved house and needed only to notify the post office of their new address.

Adam Brown
6 September 2003

Design babies' prams, pushchairs and buggies with sound systems that would play back the sound effects of more exciting modes of transport while the child is being pushed. A horse-riding soundtrack would offer a gentle clip-clop through slow strolls and build to a thunderous gallop on more energetic walks. Other popular soundtracks could include racing cars and spaceships.

Mary Slim
8 September 2003

491

Install ATM cash machines with cameras that take pictures of the customers using the services. In addition to deterring fraudulent uses, simple technology could be employed to recognise a frown or a smile from genuine customers when their balances were displayed on screen and a helpful, supportive or congratulatory note could be added to the advice slip.

David Owen
11 September 2003

492

Design padded headwear for babies starting to crawl or walk. The headgear would be similar in shape to those worn by amateur boxers but obviously designed in a slightly cuter colour scheme or pattern.

Charles Addison
15 September 2003

493

Introduce central locking for houses.

Roy Walsh
19 September 2003

494

Market celebrity chef branded Microwave ovens that use voice recordings instead of an annoying beep, such as Nigella Lawson saying, 'Darling, dinners ready!' If the door was not opened after a couple of minutes the oven might also say, 'Oh come on darling, it's getting cold!' There could also be a facility for homeowners to record their own hilarious alarm messages or use the voices of loved ones if they were to be away for a long period of time or dead.

Steve Sargent
24 September 2003

495

Introduce a packaged food product called 'I don't mind', which would contain a random meal. The mystery product range would broaden public taste and would be the perfect impulse purchase for partners and children unsure of what to have for dinner.

Geoff Jones
29 September 2003

496

Open a hair salon where, instead of talking about the weather, the stylist would teach the customer something while they were cutting their hair — conversational Spanish or beginner's Descartes, for example.

Ailsa Jones
5 October 2003

Editor's note:
This idea can either be taken as the perfect compliment to Sam Torme's 'Air Cuts' or as a somewhat less daft and genuinely plausible alternative.

497

Launch a Country of the Year Awards. The award and event would be something like the Eurovision song contest without the songs, which in itself wouldn't be such a bad idea. Countries would be invited to produce short films to be screened on television and nominate key nationals to answer questions in a studio discussion before a global audience voted for their favourites.

Mary Slim
17 October 2003

498

Editor's note:
This is a great idea which may just have arrived a little late given the rapid adoption of digital photography

Install a mobile one-hour photo lab in a truck or trailer. The portable lab would tour events such as festivals, races and such like.

Joseph Lansing
21 October 2003

499

Introduce false but realistic chewable nails that would allow nail biters to feed their habit without causing damage to the real nails underneath. The false nails could possibly be flavoured - strawberry or salt and vinegar, perhaps.

Clark Edwards
27 October 2003

500

Erect meeting posts in city centres. The posts would be arranged in a wide circle and would be called 'One o'clock', 'Two o'clock', and so on. People could simply arrange to meet Four o'clock and safe in the knowledge that all parties would be aware of the time and location of the rendezvous. To make things even simpler, Twelve o'clock' would be due north and Six o'clock due south.

Chas Bayfield
30 October 2003

Editor's note:
Anyone left waiting at a meeting post could always wander down the road to Ten Past or Twenty Past to see if their late friends were loitering there.

POSTSCRIPT:
THE ONE THAT GOT AWAY

I wrote the introduction to this book in August 2003. Idea A Day had been up and running for three years during which time over 1,000 ideas had been published. Myself and my partners in the site were confident that we had created something unique and of value. Whenever we talked to anyone about Idea A Day, however, we would invariably be asked what we had achieved and, unfortunately, simply replying that we had kept a website online since the year 2000 or that we had a book coming out in 2004, just didn't cut it. People wanted to hear about ideas that had 'been done', and done in such a way that they might have heard of them. Writing the introduction, I couldn't imagine that readers of this book would think any differently.

As it happened, it was in August that Jay Pond-Jones, an Idea A Day subscriber since day one, invited me to attend a meeting at the marketing group Chime PLC. Jay had previously been the creative director of a number of London advertising agencies and had recently been appointed Head of Content at Chime. Part of his brief was to explore new ideas and angles for television, with a particular regard to developing advertiser funded programming. Chime were already working with David Brook, a television executive, who had been the marketing director of *The Guardian* and Channel 5 and most recently Director of Strategy at Channel 4. David was planning a move into the world of multi-channel television, where the bingo channel Avago and The Thomas Cook Channel had begun to demonstrate that companies and brands could make television and make money without relying solely on traditional advertising. Chime wanted to position themselves at the forefront of this new era of digital interactivity and were looking for an idea to take them there.

I went to the meeting armed with four A4 pages of closely typed ideas, mainly pulled from the Idea A Day archive. Jay introduced me to David and we went through the pages. It took about 10 minutes to find an idea we liked and another 50 minutes to determine that it would actually work. The idea was from Idea A Day and had been published on 13 February 2001. It was Chas Bayfield's idea for a television channel on which a panel of experts would recommend to viewers what they should be watching on all the other channels. The idea had been on the site for more than two years without attracting any interest from anyone. Nestled amongst a thousand other concepts of varying purposefulness and insight, it had been no more than another clever twist of an idea - as much a neat joke as a business plan. Singled out in a meeting with a brilliant television marketer and a PLC with major company clients and money of its own to invest, it became quite an exciting property indeed. Confident that we had cracked it, Jay determined to propose the idea within Chime, David left to consider the financial viability and the funding required and I volunteered to write a creative treatment, give it a name and, of course, call Chas.

Flipside TV
It took about a month before the meetings I had on the project with Jay and David began to be populated with other interested parties and for decisions to be taken that would actually be put into practise. I had come up with the name Flipside fairly quickly after the first meeting and Jay and I had written up content ideas to fill hours of television. I had also asked Chas to let me run with the idea on the understanding that I would give him half of anything I could hold onto. Chas was happy to be a sleeping partner; he and I both had a

number of projects on the go and he was working flat out to keep his own advertising agency, Arkwright International, in business. Jay had pitched Flipside to his bosses at Chime and the CEO, Chris Satterthwaite, and the Chairman, Lord Tim Bell, were enthusiastic supporters. He had also introduced the idea to James Brown, the founder of *Loaded*, ex-editor of *GQ* and publisher of *Jack* magazine, who was keen to get involved. David Brook had worked up a number of different options for funding and launching the channel and also attached Richard Bacon as a presenter and executive producer.

At the end of September David Brook came to a meeting with a radical plan. In addition to his work with Chime, he was also acting as a consultant to a new television company planning to launch a games and competition channel called GameNation that was to be funded by telephone revenues. Every business plan we had written for Flipside as a channel in its own right showed a shortfall of about £1m, which would need to be underwritten by advertising or sponsorship of some kind. David had prepared a deal for GameNation to broadcast Flipside for two hours a night, five nights a week. The channel would take an equity position in return for providing a studio and all facilities. All we had to do was be ready to go on air in three weeks.

Flipside launched on 20 October 2003 on the Sky Digital Channel 277, sponsored in part by The Carphone Warehouse, a Chime client. As of January 2004, it is still on air broadcasting live from 8 - 10pm on what is now called Nation277. Richard Bacon presents on a regular basis and Chas' panel of experts are just that, three media personalities sat in front of three televisions, recommending to the viewers what they could be watching or should be watching at that very moment. Whenever a guest finds a channel or programme they are excited about, the producer brings it up for the viewers to see, with Flipside providing the commentary.

On the nights when it's working well (and hopefully they are becoming more frequent) it's hard to believe that such a show never existed before. It's as though Flipside jumped though a loophole in the fabric of television. Whether it is as, 'a human programme guide', 'a live listings magazine' or 'the programme that does the flipping for you', Flipside has become one of the most written and talked about shows on digital television. Of course, it has to work as well as a business as it does as a television show and there is no guarantee that Flipside will still be on air when this book is published.

Writing in *The Sunday Telegraph* in November 2003, the journalist Giles Smith neatly summed up the show's prospects,

"The post-modern implications of [the show] could take a decade or so for some full-time media studies graduate to work out. By which time Flipside will either have long been consigned to television's ever more capacious dustbin or will be the only thing that anyone really cares to watch. Right now I'm not entirely sure. I'll get back to you on this in a decade."

Hopefully in ten year's time, many more ideas from this book will be in evidence.

David Owen
January 2004

INDEX OF CONTRIBUTERS